OWNING YOUR CHOICES

STORIES OF COURAGE FROM 8 INSPIRATIONAL
WOMEN AROUND THE WORLD

COMPILED BY
MARSHA VANWYNSBERGHE

Owning Your Choices Copyright © 2020 by Marsha Vanwynsberghe

All rights reserved. No part of this publication may be reproduced, distributed or transmitted in any form or by any means, including photocopying, recording, or other electronic or mechanical methods, without the prior written permission of the publisher, except in the case of brief quotations embodied in critical reviews and certain other noncommercial uses permitted by copyright law.

This book is for entertainment and education purposes only. It is not intended to serve as business or life advice. This book is not intended to instruct or advise in any way. Using any of the information in this book is based on the reader's own judgement after consulting with his or her trusted professionals. The views expressed herein are not necessarily those of the publisher, nor the other co-authors.

Published by Prominence Publishing

www.Prominencepublishing.com

ISBN: 978-1-988925-66-0

Table of Contents

Foreword i
Introduction 1
Untying the Knots of Divorce and Stepping into My Purpose – By Marisa Lupo 5
Finding The Freedom Within – By Kelly Thorne 17
Emerging Evolved – By Shannon Matthews 33
Rise Up – By Tinya Gray 43
Hungry To Heal – By Kim Basler 57
Tragedy, Truth and Triumph – By Lynn Tanguay 71
Breaking the Silence – By Thembeka Ntuli 83
Radical Responsibility Became the Light in my Dark Life – By Marsha Vanwynsberghe 95
Stay Connected 105

Foreword

There are some people whose path you cross unexpectedly, and it feels like you've known them your whole life. Those whose presence calms you and whose words seem to speak to your soul. Marsha is one of those people.

Marsha and I met at a women's summit where we were both speakers for the event. We had no prior introduction, not even so much as a conversation before we were paired as roommates. We gave each other a friendly 'let's see where this goes' kind of smile and neither of us could've predicted what came next. It wasn't before long that smiles turned into laughter, laughter turned into stories and stories turned into a sisterhood. We chatted well into the night, sharing stories of fear, freedom, and everything in between. I don't recall ever being so open and vulnerable to a complete stranger before that night. That, I would later learn, is Marsha's superpower.

That evening is one I will not soon forget, but the real standout moment was when I witnessed Marsha take the stage and move an entire audience with her calm, but rock-solid disposition. I remember looking forward to her talk but didn't think it would speak much to me. We lived such different lives and had a completely different history, after all. Boy was I wrong. That day, Marsha spoke about the importance of owning our choices and how doing so enables us to break free from the constant loop of an old and unserving narrative. She explained that every time we blame ourselves, every time we justify our thoughts and refuse to accept help, we add layers to the armour we carry. This armour, she continued, is our defense. We tell ourselves that we need it to keep the pain out and it becomes part of us. The trouble, you see, is that armour doesn't just keep out the bad. It keeps out the good; the support, the healing, the opportunity to make a lifelong friend at a conference.

It was as if she was speaking directly to me. I carried the weight of my armour for longer than I'd realized, until it crushed me, and I had no choice but to put it down. My armour was made up of all the "shoulds". Who I thought I should be, what I thought I should be, where I thought I should be in this stage of my life? My armour made me strong, tough love is what was keeping me going, I told myself. Every "should" that crept into my mind added more weight. I built a barricade around myself and ultimately kept myself stuck in a story that was not actually mine. As it turns out, I had masterfully built walls to keep out who I really was and what I really wanted. Pursuing the real vision I had for myself terrified me. I would need to face parts of myself that I would rather ignore. I would need to take responsibility for things I'd deflected for so long. I would need to accept that I was exactly where I was because of the choices I made, no one else. But the alternative was living a life that was not mine, so I began to put my armour down. With each piece I lowered, I learned more about myself. The more I learned, the more I shared and the more I shared the more free I felt. Sharing parts of me, the real me, has opened doors I would've never imagined. My best-selling book, my TEDx talk, my podcast and every opportunity in between, is a direct result of me owning my story and sharing it with those who needed to hear it. Marsha's words served as the encouragement I needed to keep forging my path.

By allowing ourselves to be seen, we create an environment for others to feel comfortable coming forward and speak their truth. Only in the exchange of our thoughts, emotions and lived experiences can we create a global impact.

My hope for you dear readers, is that the stories of the women featured in this book will inspire you to write the next chapter of yours. May you remain curious about what's possible and put your armour down just long enough to let hope in. Change starts here, if you let it.

Samantha Kris
International Speaker, Success Coach & Best-Selling Author
514-250-9718
www.samanthakris.com
LinkedIn | Podcast | TEDx talk | Bossing Up Community

Introduction

Before you dive into these incredible stories, it's important that I share a little bit about myself and how this book came to life. Actually, truth be told this book was my inspired idea 4 years ago, long before I wrote my own book, and I am so grateful to finally see it come to life.

For years I was a mom trapped in a story of dealing with teen substance abuse at a level that was far past any level of experimentation. For years we struggled with our two teen boys with substance abuse that affected all areas of our lives including, school, jobs, sports, family, extended family, police, criminal charges and eventually living arrangements. It was a period of my life that was a blur of pain, heartbreak and truthfully learning some of my most powerful life lessons. I had to learn how to forgive myself and others, how to own my choices, take radical responsibility for myself, and learn to let go of anything outside of my control. It was no easy feat.

I started to share my story in closed Facebook groups and on stages in small venues, and it was then that I truly started to realize that I was not alone. The world was full of others who also shared stories of struggle, shame, guilt, and pain. The more I realized that I wasn't alone, the more it fueled me to continue to share my story. If I could put a purpose to my pain, it completely changed my outlook and gave me hope. This in turn inspired me to share to give others hope in overcoming their stories.

I had a dream of writing my own book to share my story, yet I couldn't figure out where to start.

In 2016 I joined a collaborative book project and it was the first time sharing my story in print. It opened my eyes to the power of collaboration. I'd spent years fighting the cycle of shame on my own and completely isolating myself from others. Working with others to all share our stories allowed me to grow my courage. I wanted to create a space and a platform for women to share their stories, and I felt that I would be "ready" to pursue this possibility by first writing my own book. In 2017, I wrote my book, "When She Stopped Asking Why", which became a 6X Bestseller and exceeded all of my expectations. This book opened my eyes to the possibility of creating a platform to help women to call out their stories while learning how to take ownership of their stories and learn to share them with the world.

In 2017, I started my podcast, "Own Your Choices Own Your Life" and through the process of sharing my podcast, it reached other countries worldwide, like Africa. Through the podcast, my book, and social media, I connected with a young woman from Africa who had an incredible story to share. In 2019, this motivated me to look at bringing the collaborative book idea to life. Life took many unexpected turns between 2019 - 2020 including lost jobs, personal, health challenges, and the global pandemic of COVID. I am so excited to finally see this book come to life.

This book represents inspirational stories of courage from women who have overcome unbelievable stories. I know that you will feel connected to the women who committed to sharing their stories of how they owned their choices, leading to truly owning their life. May their stories of strength, courage, and power inspire you to know that at any time, you can also change your story.

Know that the road of struggle becomes the road of growth, and your story can lead you in directions you never planned and causing you to meet the people who were meant to be on your path. You are here for a reason, you have gifts wrapped up in your story that can impact, serve, and support others. Don't keep those gifts to yourself. Learning how to unlock those gifts may ultimately be the freedom you have been searching for all along.

With massive amounts of love and gratitude,
I see you and you are powerful.

Marsha Vanwynsberghe
Speaker, Coach, and Author
Own Your Choices

"You're not a victim for sharing your story. You are a survivor setting the world on fire with your truth. And you never know who needs your light, your warmth, and raging courage."
— Alex Elle

Untying the Knots of Divorce and Stepping into My Purpose

By Marisa Lupo

The journey back to me began in my late 30's. It was the tail end of my 19-year relationship: fifteen years of marriage with two children, a life that most women dream of, and one big entangled Italian family.

Where do I even begin? How does one begin to share a story that at the time seemed so disconnected, so robotic, so lifeless? It hurts me to my core to recall it; to remember all the ways in which I neglected my spirit in order to be "the good girl". The girl who did anything and everything to not rock the boat, the girl who lived a life that marked all the boxes on her checklist.

What was there to complain about? I had all the things that I thought would give me the life I dreamed of. I married my high school sweetheart, our Italian families would come together for many celebrations, I obtained my BS in business management, had two beautiful children, became a successful real estate investor, built our very own custom dream home, took exotic vacations around the world, and I even had my own "Sex in the City" circle of amazing girlfriends. We had all the material possessions I could ever imagine. Life was carefree.

But on the inside, I was anything but carefree.

Let me skip ahead to my "dark night of the soul." The night where nothing made sense anymore and when my life felt meaningless. I felt as if I could have been in a room of a hundred people, yet nobody could see me, the real me. A ghost, that's who I was. I didn't even recognize myself anymore. I didn't understand why I felt so empty. Why was I going through the motions without any emotion?

On this night the inner critic came in like a hurricane. 'You didn't think this was going to be easy, Marisa, did you? What are people going to say? Who the hell do you think you are asking for a divorce? No good mother leaves their children's father.' Guilt, my constant companion, my dirty little sidekick. Guilt was the glue that kept me in my marriage. It may have been the glue that kept generations of women before me from being stuck in situations that no longer served them.

Up until this moment I had been the Queen of convincing myself, to the point that I believed in my own betrayal. I was drowning in a sea of expectations, living a life that wasn't mine, unable to differentiate my own desires. I felt like a complete fraud, and in a pivotal moment of desperation, I begged for a sign of life. 'This can't be it for me! There has to be more!'

The power that I had over convincing myself was mind-blowing.

December 6, 2012

It was the morning after my dark night. I was 37 years old, still living with my soon to be ex-husband and two children, awaiting the commencement of our divorce, and I never felt more alone. I was completely unsupported by my family in my decision to leave my marriage. The darkness in my eyes revealed the shell of a person that I had become.

There's something about being in the eye of the storm. They say that the eye of the storm is so calm because the strong surface winds never reach the center. Little did I know my soul knew to retreat away from the outside chaos, inward towards the only place I felt safe. The minute I retreated to this place was the moment I found my truth.

It was that morning that changed everything for me. If I had any doubts about being alone, it vanished in seconds. As I sat on my bedroom floor blow-drying my hair, a different question echoed deep inside me: 'Who was Marisa before all of this – and how did she lose herself? How did I lose track of the dream I had as a child, the deep desire to live a life devoted to helping other people?'

While I have always felt God's voice speaking to my heart in quiet whispers, now, this presence came storming in like a bolt of lightning I could not ignore. Suddenly, I felt this massive force of energy blast through my chest. It took me a minute to catch my breath. I experienced a sensation I can only describe as something like a computer program downloading into my heart. I called out, "God is this you?" Hearing nothing, I began to weep from the sense of this powerful force.

At that moment none of it made any sense. 'Why now? Why did this energy, this force, this knowing, God, why did it feel the need to meet me at the eye of my storm?'

I can't even begin to explain why my experience happened or what it means, but what I know for certain is that there was an internal knowing that was loud and clear. There was no ambiguity in the message. What was removed from my being was guilt and shame, and the message that I received was that these emotions were standing in the way of my purpose.

The veil had been lifted and the darkness was drowned out by the light. The quiet voice whispered, "You cannot do what I need you to do if you continue to carry what isn't yours."

What I know for sure is that I am not special or unique. At that moment I was just ready: ready to let go of control, ready to let go of living a lie, ready to give up the checklist, and ready to trust what I had neglected for way too long...my inner spirit.

Despite the chorus of disapproval, disappointment, and hostility from my family and even some friends, I separated from my husband and began the process of taking back control over my life. I was armored with a strong knowing that there was something bigger for me than the small box I put myself in.

I don't want to be defined by all the ways my divorce paralyzed me, but let me just say that divorcing with children in an entangled family was extremely messy, especially when my wounds were wide open and being that at the time I was unaware of all the ways in which I neglected myself. It was and is one of the most difficult experiences I have ever had to endure. It tested every fiber of my being, and it was also my saving grace that at the time I could not see.

My divorce was my crucifixion: I knew it had to be done, I knew I would have people turn their backs on me, and I also knew it wasn't my job to worry about how it made others feel as long as I stood in my truth. I was standing in my conviction, walking through the darkness, but guided by the light. Guided towards my purpose.

Taking back my power was no small feat, yet I knew that in order to take my freedom back I would have to fight for the unconditional love and acceptance my soul craved. I was terrified of going backward and putting myself back in the cage that I once built for myself.

Then things got even harder: lawyers, divorce courts, custody hearings, court counselors, opinionated families that were living in comparison, fear, and lack...this is what was waiting for me on my journey towards unraveling my marriage.

What I recognized was that my own healing was never going to be dictated in a courtroom, by a judge, or by anything being mandated by anyone. This system kept both of us in our ego and created a deep desire to win at all costs. What either of us had yet to realize was that there are no winners in divorce, only opportunities to heal or to stay stuck in a victim mindset.

I chose to heal, even when it meant I had to give up everything. I had to give up the need to blame, the need to be right, the need to win, the need to defend myself as a woman, the need to protect my ego and my image, the need to be a 'perfect' mother, the need to be responsible for anyone else's happiness, the need to judge anyone or anything.

Just when I thought I had surrendered to everything; I was proven wrong. At almost 15 years old my son felt it was in his best interest, for many reasons, to go and live with his dad. Every part of my being was devastated, once again. I thought, 'How in the world is this still happening? What does this say about me as a mother? How can his dad support taking "my" son away from me? How did we become these people?'

Recalling this time in my life still carries great sadness. How can someone that came from me, through me, who intimately was mine for nine months, nourished by my own body, be taken away to fill the ego of another? My heart still bleeds. But the strength I had inside me to rise above any attempt at tearing me down was victorious.

At just 15 years old my eldest son helped me heal the deepest and darkest shadow side of myself. He single handedly taught me the lesson that my soul was longing to heal: my deep wounds of comparison, of control, of not enough-ness. The divorce did not cause this. This was childhood trauma that was left untreated, and at the time I desperately needed my son to make me feel whole. I needed him to remind me that I was needed and loved, that this wasn't just a competition between his dad and me. That he needed me too.

We worked with court counselors who tried to fill the gap between us, as well as our own private counselors, and we got nowhere. Ultimately, it was a battle for who had the strongest ego, and who was willing to turn themselves inside out in order to be able to keep their pride intact.

Once again, here I was, still in the same old survival pattern of needing to defend myself and needing to prove myself worthy. Not only had I done this in childhood and my marriage, but now I was defending myself as a mother. 'Oh, hell no, Marisa! When are you going to learn?!' These were the thoughts screaming in my head. I needed to heal because nothing on the outside was going to do it for me.

This was not my son's burden to bear. This was my internal work, yet unconsciously I was throwing my wounds on his shoulders. Through my son, I found the courage to face my dark shadows, the ones left lingering from childhood. I never thought that through such pain, such despair and hopelessness, I would find unconditional love and healing, not only for my son but for myself.

There is NOTHING on this earth more powerful, more healing, more sacred than a mother's unconditional love for her children. Believe me when I tell you it was hard as hell to love somebody that knew how to trigger my deepest darkest fear, but true love has no container, it has no restraints, it has no requirements other than to love somebody at a cellular level. The love that I have for my children stretches beyond time, beyond taking score, beyond them needing to fulfill any of my own needs.

Untying the knots of divorce started with knowing that before I was a wife, before I became a mother, I was a person. A person that deserved to love herself completely, a person that deserved to know she was already whole, a person who was put on this earth to follow her own path and her own purpose, a person that had her own identity. I needed to come back to that reality in order to remember who I was and what I needed to fulfill in this lifetime.

Strand by strand, I had to untie all the knots. The knots of what I was told things should look like. I had to let go of people and things that no longer served me. I had to forgive those in my life that were living unconsciously. I forgave myself for buying into beliefs that weren't my own. I had to let go of the need to please others at the cost of neglecting my spirit. I had to let go of trying to control anything or anyone. I had to let go of the need to compare myself to anyone. I freed myself of any guilt and shame that I carried around like an anchor. I let go of the need to defend my choices and actions. I let go of trying to be the perfect anything...especially the perfect mother.

One by one, untying every knot has been part of the journey, and it continues to be. Every day it's a practice. Every day I journey within and have deep-rooted conversations, the ones where my voice meets my spirit and their conversation is stillness. That stillness is where my truth lives, it is the only truth that exists.

As crazy as it sounds, I am grateful that I wasn't supported, that I was questioned and criticized. I would have never found my inner strength, courage, and my true voice.

In becoming a butterfly, the caterpillar must go through the painful process within, on its own, without any help from the outside world in order to transform and emerge into its true essence. This is what I call Butterfly Magic. The magic came from going inside, no matter what was happening in the outside world, and emerging into the beautiful creation I was meant to be.

Once I was ready to untie all the knots and emerge out of the cocoon and really step into my power...well this was where my life's work began.

I realized I needed support. The cage I created for myself didn't have the necessary tools I needed to get out. I sought after counselors and coaches. I found mentors virtually because they were far and few between in my circle. I read books, I went to women's retreats, I created new friendships that supported my journey, I listened to podcasts, and I became a certified coach. I did anything and everything to empower myself, and even when I didn't feel powerful, I let this virtual family that I created hold me up until I could do it alone. And I did it all with grace and compassion for myself. I wasn't in a race to some imaginary finish line. There is no finish line.

I do not want my legacy to be generations of knotted strings that tie us all together. This is not the right condition for a butterfly to take flight. It is my offering as a conscious parent to detach and set free what isn't mine. They say our children are our greatest teachers. I learned this the hard way. Children come into the world bearing the greatest gifts, and I am so grateful.

Without a dark night of the soul, without complete surrender, without disruption of monotony there would have been no change. I would not have been able to set myself free and embrace my Butterfly Magic had I not bit by bit, and strand by strand untied the knots that kept me from my true essence, which was to emerge into my purpose of helping other women find their own true essence. This is my work, my purpose- to now coach women to find their own Butterfly Magic.

About the Author

Marisa Lupo is a certified life coach who has mastered strategies that empower women in her private practice to cultivate an authentic life overflowing with love, meaning, and passion. Graduating with a degree in business management, she quickly became a successful real estate investor of over 15 years. After having checked all the boxes that Marisa thought were going to lead her to the happiness she craved, something deep within her was still missing.

Unfulfilled with passion, she left her career to follow a life of meaning. Purpose emerged through her most challenging time; an entangled divorce with two children, a very opinionated Italian family, without much support from those closest to her. She developed the tools and strategies to untie the knots of divorce that bound her and started living a life of freedom. In her coaching, Marisa guides women through untying the knots of divorce and teaches them how to emerge into their highest self.

Finding The Freedom Within

By Kelly Thorne

Thoughts are deceiving, aren't they? I thought I was a smart girl, a good, educated girl. I was the quiet girl you sat next to in class. This is what I thought about myself, but it was not at all how I felt about myself. What you didn't know was how awkward I felt or how uncomfortable I felt in my own skin. Never knowing what to say or how to act. I felt like by just being myself, that I wouldn't be enough. I wouldn't be liked, adored, or accepted. Perhaps you would judge me, criticize me, and worse yet, not like me with all my insecurities, fears, and flaws. It was then that I put up my very first shield. The first of many to come. I began to build my armor of aloofness, toughness, and disconnectedness. What you didn't know was how desperate I was for your approval, your acceptance, and your love.

I learned at a young age how to conform. I learned that it was safer to blend in, not to make a fuss, not make waves, to be seen, and not heard. It was easier that way. There was less chance for rejection. It was comfortable. I was comfortable, yet trapped at the same time, because deep down something was burning inside me that said you don't need to do this.

It's ok to be yourself, you don't need to hide.

But I did. I continued to become a chameleon and be the person I thought everyone wanted me to be.

I wasn't entirely sure who I wanted to be though. So, I tried to guess. I continued to bend and conform and make assumptions on what "Kelly" was required to show up.

Was it the good girl at church? The respectful daughter at home? The outgoing friend? The party girl at night? The sensual lover?

I often kept my opinions, my beliefs, and my thoughts to myself. At a young age, I found my release through writing. That was where I found my first escape. In time I discovered alcohol which gave me the false courage to say whatever my heart desired to whomever I desired.

Being the good girl, the nice girl, the quiet girl is exhausting especially when you have so much you want to say. Conforming to people and places, never truly allow you to become who you are meant to be. I began to adopt behaviors and attitudes that were never mine, to begin with. I had nudges and pulls to how I wanted to be and how I wanted to show up in this world but at the time that seemed boring to me. I was craving excitement. I was craving something different. I was like a free spirit trapped in a body of conformity.

This is where the endless and unforgiving battle of people-pleasing began. If I do something for you and you give me the attention I was so desperately craving, then I felt worthy. If you stroked my ego, I would come back begging for more. The only problem with this for someone like me is that it is never enough. I was trying to fill a void, an emptiness so deep inside me that no amount of attention, people-pleasing, love, adoration, drug, or sex could heal.

Despite coming from a good home and having parents who loved and adored me, it never seemed to be enough. I had the disease of perception. The disease that never allowed me to see things as they were. The one that allowed me to play the victim for much of my life. The one who continued this belief that I wasn't enough. I wasn't good enough, smart enough, talented enough, pretty enough, strong enough. I wanted to be rescued. To be swept off my feet.

I truly believe that you can be presented with all of life's opportunities, but if you don't have the self-confidence or self-worth to believe in yourself and that you are deserving of more you will find yourself in places you never knew existed.

As thus begins my journey into addiction.

This is the foundation for how I went from everyone's "Good Girl" to "How the hell did I end up here kind of a girl?".

The kind of roller coaster ride that leaves you thinking..." This is NOT my life, this CANNOT be my life" and then with one swift glance in the mirror I am reminded that yes, "Yes, Kelly...This is you."

"This is all you."

The simple task of looking in the mirror became incredibly difficult as the years went on. I couldn't confront the person standing there. I couldn't look her in the eyes. I wouldn't look her in the eyes. I didn't love her. I didn't honor her. I sure as hell didn't respect her. I didn't know her anymore. I had let myself down. I was living a lie. My secrets, my lies, the show I put on, made me feel like a hypocrite every single day. I was crawling inside my own skin. I felt trapped. Wishing some days to go to sleep and never wake up again. Everything that I knew I stood for but was too afraid to express had vanished. What I did know, even on the darkest of days was that I was not lost, not entirely anyway, I just needed to find my way back to myself. A route that seemed so dark and bleak at one point began to brighten on the horizon.

My desire to be accepted, loved, and not rejected was so strong and powerful that I was willing to do whatever I could to chase that feeling. That feeling alone tore me apart. I chased it for so long and so vigorously that I lost sight of who I was and why I was here.

Wanting you to like me, to love me, meant doing things that compromised my values. If I had a boyfriend, I wanted yours too. If you had a girlfriend, it was game on. Jealousy ran deep though my veins, and what I had was never enough. If one boyfriend was good, two must be better. This pursuit while exciting at the time, also became my addiction. Never satisfied, never enough, I always wanted more. I wanted to be desired and was willing to do whatever it took. When I felt desired, I felt like I could move mountains. I felt invincible. I felt like I was walking on water. I chased that feeling, but it never lasted. If you are always chasing it from an external source, the chase will never end.

It was no surprise that when I met the man I was to one day marry, I was drawn to the riskiness of it all and the wild and unpredictability that came with him. He was loud, he was bold, he was electric, and he could light up a room just by showing up. It's not surprising to me that when we met, he ignited everything that laid dormant inside of me. What I didn't know was that he was chasing the same feeling himself.

He was everything that I wasn't, and while it appeared that he had everything I wanted, I later found out that this persona was his way of protecting himself. We were two broken people trying to make a whole. We were trying to complete all those broken pieces and fill all those voids that we couldn't do ourselves.

I tried to be the perfect wife, play the part, go to all the events, the parties, smile when I didn't want to be there, or when I was too tired to be there. Agreeing to the things that I felt strongly against just because I was afraid of conflict or worse yet stone-cold silence.

I grew up in a home where silence was prevalent. Walking on eggshells with every step. To me, that is worse than anything I have ever experienced. That gnawing in the pit of your stomach that something just isn't right. Despite how horrible that made me feel, I was then to go on to repeat the same patterns that I witnessed as a child. I will never forget the look on my daughter's face after we had just finished one of our fights and I thought to myself, NO. NO! This is not how she is going to think a marriage should be. This is not how two humans should talk and communicate with each other. This is NOT going to be a pattern I plan on repeating. I spoke those words to myself and knew in that instant something had to change.

> *"If nothing changes, nothing changes."*
> *Courtney C. Stevens.*

It was time to get off the ride.

Our lives had become so broken and so shattered that I had no idea how to pick up the pieces. Our marriage had fallen apart and was beyond repair. My life as I knew it had fallen apart. I tried to do everything in my power to fix that which was beyond my control, without realizing I had to start with myself.

It was time to face the reality of what was. I just wasn't ready for that yet.

Addiction, drugs, and alcohol had become a significant presence in our house as we were both trying to escape from our own problems. As the addiction grew so did my reliance on alcohol. It was the only way I knew how to cope. It was the only way I knew how to find peace. (That peace came from the first few glasses of wine. Then to make sure I was blocking out every feeling, every emotion, every pain, I added in a few shots of vodka, which in all likelihood was a bottle a night in order to completely numb out all pain. I teetered between not wanting to go to sleep because I knew I would have to face another day tomorrow and then fantasizing of passing out and praying to God that morning would never come for me again.

I find solace now that God gave me his Grace to continue.

I would often find myself on the cold bathroom floor, or collapsed in the corner of the shower, weeping at what my life had become. They say courage comes to you in a variety of ways, for me, it came from a whisper. A whisper saying, "Not now Kelly. This is not your time. Your kids need you and you need them." The insanity of all this was that this was an ongoing dialogue, many nights of this, many early mornings of scraping myself together. For many it's never a one and done thing... it's continuously beating ourselves up because we are afraid of what it looks like to execute that courage. These whispers continued until one day in the cold of winter I was knocked to my knees.

I was living in fear and doing all I could to just survive. I was suffocating and didn't know how to save myself. I had crumbled inside and didn't know where to begin to ask for help. I was still wearing the mask of a good girl, wife, daughter, and mother. Failing in every area, yet still wondering what people would think of me. What would they think of my family?

Acceptance and belonging were still driving forces for me; however, I had isolated myself so much that I had none of these.

Drugs and addiction swept through our house, slowly at first, and then like wildfire, destroying everything and everyone that stood in its way. Attempts to make it stop, to go away, were always met with resistance. Drugs stole our hearts, our souls, and left shells of us behind. Drugs stole everything of value that we ever owned. Paying bills became a nightmare, loss of utilities a common affair. Negotiating with collection companies and using excuses for a poor business year became par for the course. Knocks at our door woke me in the middle of the night. Afraid to answer, more afraid of the repercussions of not answering. Still trying to make things look normal from the outside. Absenteeism from work was at an all-time high. Hiding my car in the garage after driving my kids to school late was predictable. Always sick, always with a migraine, always nauseous. Going to a family doctor with concerns of low iron, depression, anxiety, seasonal affective disorder, you name it, I was blaming it.

Always looking for another way out. Never being completely honest with how things were.

Drugs stole the fragmented people that we were and left pieces of dust behind.

In my vain attempts to try to manage, control, and fix someone else's addiction I failed to see that I was also part of the problem. I didn't see that I had addictive behaviors, patterns, and addictions of my own.

The guilt and shame that were so prevalent were layered with anger, fear, frustration, and anxiety.

You desperately want to ask for help because you feel powerless and hopeless, but by doing so you would have to reveal your own involvement. I wasn't ready to take ownership at this point because I believed I wasn't at fault. I was still the victim. The multiple masks and shields I had armored myself with over the years might have to come off. There was to be no more hiding.

Was I ready to unveil that person who was hiding underneath?

Did I have the strength for that? Did I have the courage for that?

My marriage that had appeared "perfect" on the outside had become a nightmare that I couldn't escape from. I had stopped being a friend to people long ago, mostly because I had too much to hide. In my quest for being liked and accepted and feeling that I could never show my true vulnerabilities, I began to isolate. Disappearing as a friend was much easier than showing up, being real, and being seen. In this space, it becomes a very lonely place. When you are hanging on by a tiny piece of thread and mustering up all the strength you must get through just one more day it can feel like the loneliest place on Earth. People are swarming all around you, but you are too afraid to let them in and ask for help. So, you continue, until one day you must make a choice. There are no options left.

> *You will never know how strong you are until being strong is the only choice you have.*
> *~ Bob Marley*

Life is funny sometimes. You fall into these patterns, which you refuse to repeat and yet somehow you find yourself making and repeating the same mistakes. Sometimes, you need to learn your lessons, one, two, three times before they click, and you say to yourself, NO MORE. I had many final awakenings in that last year. Many times, where my life came to a crashing halt, and in the wee hours of the morning after yet another sleepless night I found myself begging, pleading for mercy. My NO MORE came on that cold hard ground one morning in April. The ice and snow still scattered all around me, scraping my knuckles on the cold hard concrete in a failed attempt to extract my car keys which were sinking to the bottom of the frozen pool. It was at that moment that my life came to a crossroads and things started to unravel in front of me. I could continue on the way things were and watch my life crash, burn, and hit a further bottom, or I could wake myself the FUCK up, pick myself up off the ground and realize that no one, I repeat, NO ONE is going to do this for me. No one was coming to save me.

It was at that moment that I realized I had a choice. I always had a choice. I was choosing this.

What happened next was my quest for something different. My quest became not how am I going to fix him, rather yet, how am I going to fix myself. The only life I could save was my own.

I began to search for answers, I began to search for the magic pill that would change my life.

What I discovered was that there was no magic pill, there was no way around this. I had to go through it. I had to stop running with the storm, turn, face it, and go through it. I had to learn about all the things I didn't know. I had to be open, willing, and ready to receive the hard truths about my life. My teachers came from a variety of sources. I began with Google. Google over the years became my safe resource. I could read what I wanted that pertained to me, or truthfully everyone but me. This did nothing to create change. It did not address my issues or hold me accountable. It did bring a surface level of awareness though. I began the journey through a myriad of psychologists, therapists, addiction counselors, and doctors. At first, my sessions began with the relentless search of finding solutions for someone else's problem. It's no wonder this got me nowhere, and I often left frustrated wondering why they weren't helping ME. Couldn't they see how much I was suffering here? I remember being annoyed when they would turn the conversation and question me and my behaviors? I felt attacked, and often never went back to that person. I was the victim here remember?! I turned to close friends and family. I began to unravel my story. I slowly, at a snail's pace, began to unpeel the layers of my life. My quest for answers brought me face to face with my addictions and my history of being codependent. To be quite honest, I had no idea what codependency was or that boundaries were even a thing. In my case, the issue of codependency presented itself first. The explanation that stood out the most for me was "Doing for others what they should be doing for themselves, even when it negatively affects your mental health, physical health, and finances" Codependency is an extensive problem and can be incredibly debilitating. So great that there are treatment programs available for those who suffer from it. Characteristics of codependency can include:

- Feeling responsible for everyone and everything and carrying large amounts of guilt and shame.

- People pleaser to the extreme and afraid to speak up due to a fear of disappointing others.

- Ignoring your feelings and needs, often numbing them out with food, alcohol, or drugs.

- Acting like a martyr, taking care of everyone else, giving without receiving, and then feeling angry, resentful, and taken advantage of.

- Perfectionist, overworked, and overscheduled.

- Controlling, nagging, and overly critical of yourself and others.

The research is extensive and is worth looking into if you feel you may need recovery in this area.

Living with addiction and loving an addict can stretch you in ways you never thought imaginable. What I believed to be helping behaviors were so detrimental to someone struggling with addiction and equally detrimental to myself. It has been said that for every addict who needs to recover, there is a family who needs an equal amount of time or more to recover themselves. Couple that with my own addictions and you have a mess made in heaven.

I had to learn boundaries. I am still learning how to develop and maintain boundaries in my relationships. I had to learn how to let go with love and start focusing on myself.

Letting go with love took a long time. It was smattered with rage, anger, denial, blame, finger-pointing, hostility, minimizing, and rationalizing. I had to make some difficult decisions and difficult choices. It wasn't just one decision or a few choices, it was a hundred million tiny choices and sometimes some big excruciating decisions that allowed me to keep putting one foot in front of the other. Continually asking myself is this the next right thing for me. Will this get me closer to or further away from my goals.

It took taking radical responsibility and ownership for every single detail of my life. I had to let go of the comfortability and stop playing the victim and hiding behind someone else's addiction.

I had to confront my addictions. I had to get real, and honest and raw. I had to act, there was no other choice. I had to learn how to live again.

There was no one to blame in all of this. Acceptance was key. Acceptance of what was and a desire to do whatever it took to move forward. By blaming everyone and everything I had given away my power. It was time to take it back. I needed to have compassion for myself. I needed to learn to love myself again. I needed to learn how to forgive. I wasn't going to be satisfied until I had unearthed everything about myself. I knew there was much work to be done. I was ready to peel back all the layers. I became ready and willing to do the work. I cleared out all the nooks and corners where shame, guilt, and remorse had been hiding. I became honest with myself and with others. Eventually, as I began to show myself some grace and understanding I realized that I did the best I could with what I knew. I didn't know what I didn't know yet.

Shame does not live within me anymore. My truth has set me free.

As I sit here and write this, my heart is full. My heart is full of gratitude for where I am and how far I have come in my journey. My journey is far from over. I am still learning; life continues to happen. The amazing thing is though, is that now I have the tools. I continue to do the work, build my toolbox, and add more tools as the need arises. I am open to change; I am open to growth and I am open to learning how to do things differently. I am learning how to connect with myself and what my soul needs. I honor myself and I love myself deeply.

My deepest desire to share with you today is that no matter how lost you feel like you are right now, you have the ability within you to find your way back.

About the Author

Kelly is an advocate for families living alongside addiction. Her mission is to help families find freedom in their own lives, remove guilt, and empower themselves on their journey of self-discovery.

In addition to being a spouse living alongside addiction, Kelly has her own personal story of addiction and recovery. Taking ownership became a central theme in Kelly's life, and when she realized the only life she could save was her own, she began to take radical responsibility for it. Every action, every reaction, every choice, every decision. When her story shifted from one of blame to owning every part of it, she truly was able to change her life, and find the freedom she was so desperately searching for.

Emerging Evolved

By Shannon Matthews

I grew up in a home full of love, support, and compassion but also alcoholism, aggression, and depression. I cannot emphasize enough how much this influenced who I became as a woman and mother. Being a parent myself now, I can't help but wonder if my parents thought they were doing a good job. I don't want to exaggerate life in our household but as is most often the case my most prominent memories are those strongly associated with emotion. I remember parties, filled with laughter and music. I also remember the following mornings, filled with sickness and sadness. Mostly I remember the pervasive feeling of loneliness as I often seemed to get in the way of my parents. I always had the question on the tip of my tongue but didn't dare say the words out loud, "Why did you have me?" I felt like I was in the way of the lives they thought they were supposed to be living, impeding the fun they would be having if I wasn't there holding them back. Those were big thoughts and feelings for a little girl. Sometimes I felt like a burden. Sometimes I felt like an afterthought. Ever-present was the feeling of loneliness.

My father was a truck driver who went on long haul runs, and also worked internationally in Libya for the first few years of my life, so he was rarely home with us. He would drop in and out, like a recurring character on a TV sitcom. A 'larger than life' personality has never defined anyone more accurately than my father. He is a big man with an even bigger heart, his jolly appearance often equated with Santa Claus (or Kenny Rogers) and an arsenal full of thoroughly inappropriate jokes. When my dad would come home from the road there was always fanfare associated with his return. Friends and family would show up and stay late. Every night was a party at our house. When the party ended, the fighting began.

My mother struggled while my dad was away, but I was too young to fully understand. It also shouldn't have been mine to carry but unfortunately, it's still with me now. From quite a young age, I had suspected that my mother lives with some form of undiagnosed mental illness. After struggling with my own anxiety and depression, I'm now certain I was correct. Knowing that makes it difficult to look back with resentment because she truly was not capable of doing any better back then. She loved me, I knew that for sure, but there was something missing in her life and I wasn't enough to fill the void. Sadly, my mother was never treated as a priority by my father. It's hard to consider but maybe neither of us were. When I was ten years old, she somehow summoned the courage to leave the only man she had ever been with in an attempt to rebuild her life. We were so often on our own anyway I didn't expect things to be much different. In fact, I was looking forward to it because I thought if they were living apart at least my parents wouldn't fight anymore.

The years immediately following my parent's separation were tough for me. I'm not sure if this is when I began feeling like my mother's caretaker or if it was ingrained earlier. I do, however, know for certain that this was the first time my mother felt free. She seemed lighter somehow. She worked and socialized on her own terms. She began dating someone seriously and that's when I felt like I wasn't her priority anymore. When we moved in with my mother's new partner, she began to rebuild the life she thought she deserved. She made a lot of sacrifices in her marriage to my father and I wanted her to have a second chance too. I tried to be loving and supportive while distancing myself.

I was never completely comfortable with this relationship. There was this whisper I tried to ignore but, in the end, it proved to be exactly what I had feared all along. They were in a codependent relationship, both heavy drinkers who got loud and abusive when things got out of hand. I didn't spend my teenage years planning for the future, or thinking about options for education or a career. I spent every waking moment working on an exit strategy. There was an intense need to flee the dark and abusive home environment. I began working at 15 years old which served to instill a strong sense of responsibility and independence. I moved out within days of turning 18.

People who know enough about my past see a stark difference in who I should have become versus the strong and empowered woman I am now. I am often asked about how I did it and truthfully, it still baffles me. I've spent many therapy sessions reflecting on it. The closest I have to an answer is to acknowledge that from a fairly young age I was filled with sheer determination, probably ignited by a fight or flight survival instinct, not to repeat the habits and behavior that led my mother to a life of loneliness and continual betrayal. I was a first-generation high school graduate who eventually understood the power of education. I forged a new path to University and College, which ultimately led me to continue working in Academic Education.

Despite doing what I thought were all the right things, at the age of 33 I found myself in the exact situation I spent most of my life working to avoid - divorced, depressed, and now raising a child of my own under immense pressure not to screw up his life too. I felt that same void my mom was feeling so many years ago. My ex-husband couldn't fill it, my son whom I loved more than I ever imagined possible couldn't fill it, so I had almost given up looking for a remedy. At what seemed like the lowest point in my life I was faced with the greatest challenge I would ever face. To complete the picture, however, we have to go back a decade.

My mother and her partner, whom I also refer to as my stepfather, became the legal guardians of a baby boy named Logan. He was the biological child of my stepsister who was not well enough to care for him on her own. It seemed a generous and loving thing to do on their part. They were taking in their grandchild and raising him as their own. They were putting their own needs as aging adults aside to prioritize family and keep Logan from a life in foster care. They were nearing the ages of 60 and 70 at this point so I agreed to vouch for them in a meeting with Family & Child Services. I agreed that I would take on the role of legal guardian if at any point their health deteriorated. At the time I truly didn't think about the implications of this verbal agreement, but it reshaped the course of my life.

Without going too deeply into the details, I can share with you that Family & Child Services became involved in a long, drawn-out battle between my mother and stepfather. There were allegations made by both parties and regardless of the truth, I knew beyond a shadow of a doubt that Logan could not continue living in this toxic environment. The whole point of my mother and stepfather becoming his caregivers was to protect him from a life of chaos but he seemed to be even worse off than anyone had ever imagined. I could no longer stand on the sidelines nor sit in the Courthouse Gallery, hearing the details and knowing that his little life was falling apart. I intervened and offered to take him into my care. Family & Child Services accepted immediately and just like that I made the biggest decision of my life with full confidence but little preparation.

Logan moved in with my 5-year-old son and I on Christmas Day, 2015. He was just 8 years old. Imagine yourself at 8 years old. Consider the implications of leaving the people you've known as your parents, your family pets, and the only home you've ever known filled with memories of the good, the bad, and the unthinkable. Logan was always wise beyond his years and resilience was his superpower, for better or worse. Unfortunately, it sometimes led me to believe he was stronger than he was or could have been. I don't think I fully grasped the extent of his emotional needs at the time and I look back with a lot of regret. I also look back with extreme gratitude and relief that I had the wherewithal to recognize that I needed to make some serious changes for his well-being and my own.

In the earliest days of our newly formed family, it became crystal clear that I was not fully prepared mentally or emotionally. Did I do the best I could at the time? Absolutely.

I also knew that I had to do better. I had to take the steps to become emotionally intelligent, self-aware, and properly equipped to raise a child who has experienced trauma. I spent a considerable amount of time in therapy to learn how to adapt to my new role in Logan's life. I had to be honest with myself for the first time about a lot of things. I had to dig deep in order to understand the dysfunctional relationship I had with my mother. I had to dig even deeper to create the foundations of a new relationship with her while building some seriously fortified boundaries.

Logan also had to spend time with therapists, social workers, and psychologists. I didn't like that he would continue to be poked and prodded while in my care, but I also knew that it was critical to him understanding that he was now safe and secure. We did a lot of work to ensure we were rebuilding our relationships with one another on a solid foundation. Logan was eventually diagnosed with an attachment disorder, meaning that he may not ever be able to establish a healthy attachment to me in a parental role as his primary caregiver. This likely developed as the result of neglect or abuse in his formative years which devastatingly left him with the inability to trust and connect in healthy ways.

The more I learned about his attachment disorder, the more I was surprised I didn't develop something similar as a child. Then, like clouds parting, everything made sense. Who could be better suited to raise this child or help release the shame and negativity he was carrying than someone who had walked the same exact path before him? Who could be better equipped to love and care for him the way he needs than someone who was raised by the same people in the same environment and therefore knows exactly what was lacking?

It was clear that I had to interrupt the pattern of behavior that was weighing both Logan and myself down and become the person I was looking for as a child and the person Logan needed now to create a future filled with hope and possibility for our family.

It took a lot of work to have that big, bold shift in perspective, but I truly had no idea how to take action. I knew that my priority was now to advocate for Logan, who was powerless in all that was happening to his life and family, but I had to somehow reclaim my own power to be effective. A very big part of that was letting go of all the guilt and resentment I had been holding on to for far too long considering it wasn't really mine to carry. I had to stop holding my mother accountable for all the ways she let me down as a child. I had to start a fresh relationship with her now, in our newly defined roles, and as women who have grown in many ways over the last 4 decades. I had to stop blaming my mother for screwing up my life and instead take responsibility for the choices I've made, acknowledge my self-sabotaging tendencies, and give up the idea that I had to do everything for everybody. By accepting the parts of myself that I spent so much time and effort hiding, the energy in and around me began to flow freely.

I began to show up differently. Each day I gave myself permission to live authentically by sharing my true self with everyone who crossed my path. That certainly doesn't mean I spilled my guts to anyone who said "Hello" but it does mean that if someone asked how I was, I answered honestly. If I was feeling anxious, I announced it. If I was feeling sad, I cried, and asked for some time to myself. When I was feeling good about progress with Logan, I would celebrate the victories with the people who were following along on our journey. The truth is we are all connected by emotion but if we are suppressing our reality for the sake of saving face, ultimately, we are doing ourselves a great disservice. A wise and inspiring woman once asked me and a room full of women, "How can you let yourself be loved if you can't be seen?" and that was the exact moment I knew I must share my story in order to engage in life at a higher frequency.

Completely overhauling my mindset has ultimately led me to a new circle of support made up of like-minded people where we share and grow together. Some of these people were already in my life but we now relate differently because I'm showing up as the real me. I've also met new people who embrace the person I truly am without knowing the backstory, which tells me I was hiding for so long unnecessarily. The people in my life know that our relationships exist in a judgment-free space. When you invite others into a space of freedom and clarity the most magical opportunities for connection will appear. I have tapped into my creative side, spending time painting, dancing, writing, and playing music. I connect with nature on a deeper level, actively engaging in forest bathing, barefooting, and Wim Hof cold therapy to heighten my awareness. Mostly I feel compelled to challenge myself with new experiences and to pay it forward as much as possible.

I wonder now what my boys think of the life we're living? I wonder if they think I'm doing a good job. I wonder if they've noticed a change in me over the past several years. Mostly I wonder if all the good work I'm doing now is enough to wash away any residual trauma I've left them with as a result of my behaviour before I knew better. Life for us now feels very ordinary and that's the ideal. Work, school, homework, movie nights, game nights, dinner together, weekend getaways - living a life of normality was the end goal and I feel like we're on course. It will always be a work in progress but recognizing how far we've come in a relatively short period of time assures me that we're moving in the right direction. By living life in a way that emphasizes our interconnectedness through kindness, honesty, and mutual respect I am indirectly teaching Logan that regardless of attachment, he is loved.

About the Author

Shannon Matthews is a lifelong learner dedicated to self-empowerment & leading by example. While earning a History Degree from McMaster University she quickly realized that her passion was rooted in education and participation in the process. She now works as Satellite Campus Manager of Student Affairs at Conestoga College and recently completed a Post-Graduate program at UBC.

Social: @_shannonismakingthingshappen_

Rise Up

By Tinya Gray

*Just like the lotus...
We too have the ability to rise from the mud
Bloom from the darkness
And radiate into the world
—Author Unknown*

Shhhh...do you hear that? Listen again...what can you hear?

Can you hear the quiet...the soothing silence? Do you feel that aura of calm and peace all around you? If so...then well done. Seriously! That's the goal...Right?

If that is NOT what you hear at the moment, doesn't that sound lovely?

Wouldn't that be awesome to be able to close our eyes and hear and feel Peace?

Okay, Shhh...close your eyes again...now what do you hear?

Perhaps it's more like this...it's a whisper like you have to lean in and close your eyes to hear it. Or maybe it's more of a monotone conversation in your ear like a constant nagging. For some, it may actually sound like your insides are screaming at you, so loud and so constant. Which makes it impossible to hear anything because your thoughts are on total overdrive and it's SO noisy.

I totally get that. Because I too, perhaps like you, have spent a lot of time in all of these places at different points throughout my life. For many years there was so much drama in my world and this constant voice inside that wouldn't shut the heck up. It used to drive me crazy. On the outside, it looked like I had it all together. I was a fit, healthy, upbeat, fun, caring, and loving human. And I really was. But if I'm honest...that is not how I felt deep inside. I was so concerned with acceptance and what others thought about me. I was so disconnected from myself that I constantly looked outside to fill myself up, maybe you get that. I will say, I always felt that there was something within me. Like a little voice under the noise that was trying to help, to get through to me. But I stayed busy and LOUD and distracted so I couldn't hear it. Deep down I knew I had work to do, but I didn't know where to start, and opening the vault scared the crap out of me. I knew though at some point if I didn't start making changes in some way, I would never have a life I love and I would continue to live with constant noise, in trauma and drama. I felt like I was slowly dying trapped inside myself. I wanted out.

We have all heard the saying...Life is such a gift.

Right? It truly is.

Unless it feels like it isn't.

So many people spend precious time and energy in a state of suffering. Throughout my own life, there have been many breakdowns, bawling my eyes out sessions, pillow beatdowns, and literal battles with my inner self.

I know and feel in my soul the collective ache that so many share because of situations and circumstances that have been experienced. Countless people, maybe you're one of them, feel or have felt at some time abandoned, displaced, and rejected. So many souls live in constant states of shame, fear, guilt, and anger to name a few. Fewer people live in consistent positive energy spaces like love, gratitude, grace, and peace.

Did you know that you have a choice, for how you can truly live? You do.

For the longest time, I had no clue that I too had a choice.

The truth is when we are out of alignment in our lives then the Universe, God, your higher power, or whatever you believe in will give us a wake-up, smackdown, or a call in some way.

We may receive a diagnosis, lose a job, have an accident, experience a breakup, or lose a loved one.

Regardless of how painful, unfair, seemingly hopeless, or how much of a shit-show our life may feel and look, when we learn how to re-frame and re-write the stories of our lives the trajectory can completely change.

I am speaking (actually, writing) from experience. We have all heard the saying "When we change the way we look at things, the things we look at change" (~Wayne Dyer). Well it's 100% true. My life has changed and yours can too.

Let me tell you it is way more fun. Most times when I close my eyes...and I listen...I hear the peace that I spoke of above, or at least I am able to get myself there. And you deserve to have that too.

If I could sit and tell you there was only one thing that I did to remove the noise and the pain in my life, I would. There are too many things I did to count, and all the experiences and the lessons are woven together and work like a team in my life now. So, as you read on, feel it, and absorb it. If it resonates, awesome. If not, then let it go. Apply what feels right in your gut for you. You are on your journey. The personal growth journey is meant to be that. PERSONAL. You do you.

If you were to ask me the key things I have done or applied to improve my outcomes and experiences of circumstances and situations, at first, I would answer "Oh my, so many things..."

But that is not helpful if I am sharing tools and resources for you...so, here my top 5 life-changing and soul connection tips:

1) Deal with Emotion. Don't ever stuff, numb, or mask it. Let it rise, move through you, and let it go.

2) Pay attention to your intuition...our gut is also called our second brain. "Listen" with every part of you. Pay attention. Trust and Surrender.

3) Consider and acknowledge that you are not your body. You have a body and its "state" is a result of our thinking, our actions or lack thereof, and our feelings. If we treat our body in a loving way with how we feel, move, and communicate with our body, we can transcend the possibility in our body and our life.

4) Embrace breaking down, breaking through, and rising in a big way. When the tree is quiet and dormant in the winter, it does not mean that it is not growing and expanding. It is allowing itself "seasons" of growth and change to expand and show up more open, more vibrant, and stronger.

5) Acknowledge, accept, and put into action the power of Manifestation in your life...what we think about we truly bring about. We are powerful beyond measure.

Let it rise and let it go

Breakdowns to Breakthroughs

I was at a women's event once and it was ending. It had been an amazing weekend of shares and opening. I felt like a seasoned woman in the room as I had spent much of my life coaching others, in fitness, nutrition, mindset, and life stuff. I had hired and worked with coaches and I had been the coach. That weekend I focused on assisting others with their breakthroughs. Until we did a group exercise that knocked me on my knees. Literally. We were in circles of about 4 or 5 women and we were given envelopes with different scenarios inside. We each picked one envelope and had to go through how we would deal with each situation. My paper said, "You are the oldest of your siblings, your father is dying, and you have to take the lead on the funeral and the will, as well as support your family in this loss". Truth was, my biological Dad had passed a few years prior to, and I had tried to put it out of my mind since. I was a child born to teenagers, I had only seen my biological dad perhaps 10 times that I could recall. When I read this slip of paper, I immediately felt faint and dizzy. I couldn't breathe. I started hyperventilating.

I was removed from the room and looked after accordingly. I spoke with a friend about what it brought up for me, and then got over it and carried on. Throughout the weekend we had been writing notes of love, gratitude, and appreciation for each other, placing them in personalized gratitude jars we had each made to take home. Once home I read through mine and came to one note that would forever impact me and how I showed up on this planet. It said "Thank you for giving yourself space and permission to break down this weekend. I now see you as a beautiful human rather than an intimidating, perfect being – my issue not yours" Whoa. Is that how I'd been showing up? How could I help others if I was inauthentic or unrelatable? How could I help others deal with their life stuff if I hadn't yet dealt with mine? This opened a huge can of worms that obviously needed to be opened. You see there is a huge backstory to "My Dad".

When I was 9 years old, I remember my Mom sat me down and told me that my Daddy was not my Dad. BOOM. Apparently, I had another Dad, my birth Dad named Steve. My Mom was the oldest of 8 kids and life was tough. At 16 my Mom found attention, acceptance, and love in a boy named Steve. Ta-Da! I am a result of that innocent and serious young love. My parents did their best to make a start as a young couple, but it didn't work out and they separated and divorced. Mom later met my "Daddy Boo" (Bruce), the wonderful man who chose to love me and my Mom and raised me. Together they had my Sister and Brother. My parents' relationship ended up in divorce when I was 11. Throughout my life, I made up many stories and I have stuffed a ton of emotions about myself.

Think about what happens when we hold onto negative emotions: anger, guilt, shame, fear, disappointment, sadness, rejection, abandonment... you name it...eventually it comes up and out, someway somehow. And it's not pretty.

What were my stories? The voices in my head told me that I am a mistake, that my biological "Dad" didn't want me, that people don't stay, that I don't deserve, that I am a burden, that I push people away, that My Mom's life would be better without me, that I was abandoned, that I was rejected, that I'm afraid, that I should be ashamed, and it's all my fault. Those became a foundation for how I attracted, created, and showed up in my life. I believed I was dealt a shit life, and that's the way it was.

As a result, I became a people pleaser. Approval, acceptance, and acknowledgment became like oxygen for me. I wanted to make everyone happy, make them feel good. Make them like or better yet love me. I set out on a mission to be a peacekeeper and do what I thought everyone wanted me to do. What I should do. I didn't realize that all the pain I had inside was being stuffed bit by bit. I distracted myself with everyone else's needs so I couldn't feel what was coming up inside. I kept busy. I kept my surroundings noisy so I couldn't think. I attracted a boyfriend in high school that cheated. Of course, he did because, in my mind, I was unlovable. Men left me. I attracted a husband with whom we had no chemistry, no passion. Logically we were good together and we had two gorgeous sons whom I am so grateful for every day. However, the marriage was doomed because I was completely alone and lonely in a marriage. We weren't emotionally connected. I was emotionally disconnected from myself. I became a single mother because that's what I knew. When my kids dealt with drug issues as teens, I blamed myself, their father, and the community. I had so much deep stuffed emotion that was bubbling, ready to erupt at any time.

Holding onto all of that for so long and then the experience at the women's event sent my body into total shut down mode. I was self-imploding. I was exhausted and my body was gaining weight. Feeling completely blank and empty inside I had very little to give my clients and especially my sons. I went to the doctor, had all the blood work and nothing showed up. My doctor asked me if I was depressed...I said, "I am not depressed, but my body is". Then it was like a light bulb went off. I realized that I was triggered by the women's event. The note about allowing myself space and permission to break down I hadn't allowed myself space to deal with all the Dad stuff so the Universe was knocking me on my ass to deal with it. I realized that I had created this situation in my body, and only I could fix it.

There is always a compound effect.

Does this make sense to you? Have you had a situation yourself that is similar?

Ok, so what did I do?

I had to begin letting my emotions rise up and move out. I started listening to my soul when it was talking to me, taking more time for quiet and being ok with just being. I acknowledged that I was not my body, my body was a result of my feelings, thoughts, and actions or inactions. I could change the result. I learned to embrace the difficulties, the breakdowns, and the dark times as growth periods. I recognized I always came out renewed, refreshed, and ready to Rise Up in my life. I also realized that I had much more power over my life than I ever even knew. I acknowledged that much of what I had experienced, I had attracted because of my focus and my fears. I learned how to manifest in a positive way.

Specifically, I purged and cleansed my body, mind, and soul. Cleansing or purging is an extremely healthy exercise in our houses, our bodies, and our lives!

I no longer allowed myself to stuff my emotions, with distraction, alcohol, food, sex, medicine, tv, lack of activity, and people-pleasing. If I got into a thought vortex, I would change my state quickly. Sometimes I would cry, a lot, to let it move through. Sometimes I would put on loud music and dance or go out in nature and take a walk. Even now if I feel a cry surfacing, I have it, let it move through, and then carry on. We must move the energy to truly heal. I journaled a lot, I could put my unfiltered thoughts on paper and then even rip it up, burn it, or throw it away. I just had to get it all out. I also read a lot. I recognized that I could not create a new life, heal my heart and my soul by thinking, acting, and feeling the same way I had in the past. I had a lot to learn.

I also started asking myself some hard questions, 'Is what I think about Steve true? Do I really think I am a mistake? Am I a burden to my Mom?'

I focused on "what if's" ...

What if... Although I wasn't a planned pregnancy...I am one of the best things that ever happened in their life?

What if...Steve wanted to come around, but he was told not to as everyone thought it was best for me if he didn't?

What if...I CHOSE my parents for the lessons I am here to learn?

And one of the most important pieces is gratitude. Instead of going into pity, or sadness, I went into gratitude. "I am so grateful I had that experience as a child because I would not be the Mom I am if I hadn't".

I also began affirmations, like I would teach my kids. I am love, I am peace, I am here on purpose. I stopped giving energy to the fear of the future or stress of the past. I chose to surrender, faith, and presence in the moment.

The biggest change was, I wrote a new story. I now stay focused on my story, on my script of the past, present and future and I give thanks for it every day as it's true. I wrote a story about my Dads' both loving me, about my Mom loving me. My parents, like all of us, did and do the best they could with what they have. They always did. In my soul, I believed that my Dad's soul moved on when he passed. His body died, but he didn't go with it. Therefore, I chose to believe that he was free to be with me 24/7 in a way he never was before. He told me once that when I see the daytime moon, that I will know he's with me. So, he's with me always. Therefore, I haven't moved "on" from Steve. We don't have to "move on" after we "lose people". We can move forward together.

I believe that my sons chose me for the lessons they are here to learn. I love them unconditionally, yet when necessary I set boundaries and detach with love as they are on their own journey. I focus each day on what I "can do" to support them and I don't allow myself to focus on what I have no control over. I focus on their health and their safety and on them living into the best versions of themselves.

As a result of all the principles I have applied to my life, I have manifested the love of my life. I focused on what I was looking to attract into my life, and then I got to work on myself, to become who I needed to be in order to attract this man into my life. I really had to learn self-love and acceptance, peace, and grace first. As I believed, he showed up.

I choose to believe that so far, my journey in life is all a gift. In crazy ways, it has all happened "for me". That is the meaning I choose to give it ALL.

When we decide to love ourselves, eventually we understand and know that the one thing for certain is, we always have our self. There is no lack of love. There is abundance always. Everyone else is a bonus, a blessing.

Every one of us here is here on purpose. Every conversation, every experience, everything is a lesson, an opportunity, a gift. The adversity, the seemingly horrible, hard, and humbling situations are all gifts. Without any of it in this physical experience, you would not be or have become who you are. When you can let go of attachment to people, things, and the meanings, you are free to just be and to truly connect with the truth of who you are. Without judgment of self or others, you are truly free to be the incredible person you are here to be. Without justification, reasons, or excuses you are free to be your perfectly imperfect self as you are in every given moment. Without jealousy, you will realize you are enough. There is nothing you are lacking or need. When we live in the space of Jealousy, Justification, and Judgement, we dim our light and the light of others around us. We withhold love from ourselves and others. You are complete abundance, you are love, you are freedom, you are peace and you are limitless.

You are everything and you already have it all.

Big Love,

Tinya

I'd love to stay in touch and learn about your journey...let's connect...

www.tinya.love

This chapter is dedicated to my Dad, my sons' Grandpa, Bruce Boake who left us physically and is now with us forever in spirit. I would not be the Woman and Mother I am without you. Thank You Dad for all the lessons, the laughs and the love. Love You, Teen x

About the Author

Tinya Gray is a soul-based speaker, writer, intuitive guide, and visionary coach. Her work is a result of her education and experience during 30 + years as a fitness specialist and even more awakening as a woman moving through dramas and traumas of life.

Like so many, Tinya's journey as a child, woman, and a mother has been one of heartache, hurdles, and hiccups. Her life experiences of abuse, abandonment, and addiction led her on a path of many breakdowns and breakthroughs. Ultimately teaching her that changing her "script" allowed her to call in and manifest a deeper loving relationship with herself and others. Resulting in a life transformed from the inside out to one in complete alignment with her soul desires.

Helping women transcend possibility in their mind, their bodies, and their lives, growing into who they're meant to be is Tinya's true calling.

Hungry To Heal

By Kim Basler

When I Surrendered Everything Had To Change

"Our eating challenges are always here to teach us something. There is nothing "wrong" with you. Instead, get curious about what they are trying to teach you about yourself"

I went on my first diet at 12 years old and chronically dieted until I was 41. For 29 years not a day went by that I didn't stand on the scale. My disordered eating took many paths over those years and the scale went up and down like a yoyo. My high school years looked like bingeing, purging, and restricting calories. I did everything I could to try and make my body small. I learned at a young age that our bodies were meant to look a certain way. There was only one way to have a body – it was meant to be small. So I began to model the behaviours from women around me. Carefully listening to their words and adjusting my actions accordingly. I tried to resist the foods that my friends were eating and would say no to dessert-like it was the thing to do. But I could not outsmart biology. My body needed food and made sure I got it no matter how hard I tried to resist it. Then when I would eat something that I felt I shouldn't or too much of it guilt and shame would show up and I would punish my body in some way. Skipping meals. Purging. Or burning the calories off at home with exercise videos. I joined a gym at 14 and began teaching group fitness classes at 16. I loved exercising but the ultimate goal was always to burn calories and make my body look better. Fat Burners, Meal Replacement Drinks, 1-2 Day Fasting through cleansing programs, and over-exercising were my chosen strategies through my university days. I knew that purging was unsafe but all the other ways I tried to get thin or stay thin seemed like the norm. I would hear about it at the gym. Read about it in fitness magazines and saw it advertised on TV and in media sources. It seemed that every woman around me was dissatisfied with her body. I just figured I had to work at it harder. I didn't have enough "willpower" and I needed to take it up a notch – or two. I thought about what foods I can and cannot have and what I needed to do to burn off the "bad" calories all the time. These thoughts consumed me.

I was fortunate to become a mother to my daughter and son in 2003 and 2004 – what a true gift. But, I remembered struggling so much to get my weight off and get back my pre-baby body. The pressure was there because I was working full time in fitness and felt like eyes were on me to look a certain way. It was a constant battle. It's sad to say that one of my motivators for breastfeeding for as long as I did was to help get more weight off.

For years, I continued to use various diets, monitoring my weight daily on a scale, and carefully watching what I ate around people. I battled with my body and how it looked in the mirror on the regular. I often wondered what I was doing wrong. Why wouldn't my body just do what I needed it to do? Why did I literally live to gain and lose the same weight over and over? – it just didn't seem fair. I was exhausted and overwhelmed but just didn't know a way out. I felt so alone.

My life changed though in 2016 when I was working full time in a leadership position for a large fitness club chain. My drive to be perfect and always comparing myself to others made its way into my professional life. 12-14 hour days were normal on top of my daily workouts. This pressure to be all things to all people led to chest pains, sleepless nights, and hives all over my body for months. A marriage that was falling apart, a mother who was quick-tempered with her children, and ultimately thoughts of suicide. I cry now as I write this to know that my mind was envisioning me steering my wheel into other cars on the highway. Driving off a quiet country road into a large tree that could free me from the life that I could no longer keep up. My limiting beliefs were consuming me. I could no longer live this way, but I so badly didn't know how to get out. I remember on numerous occasions with my therapist saying, "If I was thinner and didn't struggle with my weight so much then I would be happier." I so deeply believed that my body was the problem. And that I was the problem. I just needed to learn how to handle the stress better in my life. I had already experienced debilitating levels of mental distress 2 other times in my life but, I would push through. I was a perfectionist, remember? I would find my way out of the chaos somehow. I would say it was a tough phase and I would get through it. I was numb to all emotions.

I remember on Christmas Day 2015 hiding out in my mother's room. I had told everyone that I wasn't feeling well and needed to lie down. That was a lie. I was emotionally numb to anything that would bring me joy and happiness. My soul was lost. I was not able to feel. I just wanted to run away and not be found.

A pivotal moment in my story was the day I decided to leave my full-time career as a fitness professional. I didn't know what I was going to do next but, I knew that if I didn't get out something bad was going to happen. For the next 40 days or so I hid. I didn't go back into the gym. I got off social media. I avoided the grocery store at all costs and I laid in my bed or on the couch. Not available for my family or myself – lost and afraid. Fear, shame, disappointment, sadness, and vulnerability ripped away at my soul, breaking me into little pieces. My career was the only thing I believed I was somewhat "good" at and now I was failing at being a wife and parent because I was unable to provide love and support for my husband and kids.

I had to surrender. The life I was living was tearing me up inside. There was no joy to be found in it and I was so very tired. No longer could I try to control every part of my life, keep all the balls up in the air, or the expectations that I had it all figured out when I didn't. It was time to remove that badge of honour that I wore so proudly. I had to face my fears and surrender and let God step in to help me find my way. It was time I listened to the whispers from my soul. Sometimes we have to go through some dark times, face ourselves in the mirror, and really look at our lives for what they are. It's messy. It requires a lot of Kleenex. A lot of tears. You will need to question everything about yourself and the choices you are making and why. It will make you want to run and hide. It's not pretty but necessary. Know this, there is peace to be found in the act of surrendering and freedom to be found on the other side if you are willing to put in the work.

It's an Inside Job – You Have All That You Need

"I realized I could keep living like a five-foot-tall piece of Velcro with giant pieces of past anxiety or anticipated future stuck to me - or I could stop."
~ Geneen Roth

When we slow down and create space, we begin to hear the whispers of the soul. Reflecting back, my soul had been whispering to me for at least 1 ½ years, sending me messages to wake up, re-evaluate my life, and how I was measuring success. I was stubborn though. Even hitting a parked car right in front of my house because I was "in auto-pilot behind the wheel" didn't work. Thankfully no one was hurt but this was my reality and there are lessons in EVERYTHING if you are willing to look for them.

I now choose to create space daily to listen to my heart and soul. And with time and patience, I have learned to trust what it's asking of me. Reflecting on my life and spending time alone has been a powerful tool because when I do this I can check in on how I am living and whether I am happy and proud of my choices. An important lesson I've learned and now teach is how we are in control of how we react and respond to each experience in our life on a daily basis. We might not always like or agree with what life throws at us, but it's up to us to respond in ways that will serve our higher good. I was always "good enough". My negative self-talk towards my body and always comparing myself towards others RULED MY LIFE. With kindness and compassion, I have learned to "water and nurture the flowers" that create a healthy mindset and allow the garden of weeds to be less attended to. This is the power of the subconscious mind...we can create a new way of being. It is absolutely possible for

YOU! I also learned through an incredible man that you will hear about soon that "I am not broken and that everything that I need is within me". Having trust and courage in my journey and believing at a soul level that I will be ok was a part of my daily gratitude. No amount of weight loss or muscle on my body would deliver this intoxicating amount of love for the woman I am. I needed to look within and listen to what my heart was asking for – it always knows what I need each day.

I can't share my journey without talking about the power of gratitude. I have noticed that slowing down my life and not over-scheduling myself has allowed me to find so many moments of gratitude in my day. I notice things that I never even used to pay attention to before. I catch myself often tearing up and wonder why? What sparked it? It's an overflowing amount of gratitude for doing the hard work. I have dug up the scars and wounds that I had buried deep in my soul and reconnected to the little girl inside of me. Sometimes this is the work that needs to be done. It isn't pretty. Emotions can happen out of the blue when you least expect it and can take you to your knees, and may require a lot of Kleenex. It doesn't matter if you are at church or in front of your entire family and friends. Emotions need to be felt – all of them. I learned this from the incredible Brene Brown. This is so important. If we choose to numb the painful emotions, we will numb the joyful emotions too.

I decided I no longer was going to numb and distract myself with food, no matter how uncomfortable I was. Or run away and bury myself in my work to avoid my life. Now, I was willing to ride the waves. If I am in a church with time for reflection and powerful moving music, sometimes the tears will start to fall like a storm that has been brewing for years. This brings with it, the most freeing feeling...no amount of weight loss brought lightness to my body like a good purge of memories, words, and tears. Our souls are begging us to dial in and listen. Now that is the kind of intentional weight loss that I celebrate because it is absolutely life-changing!

Help From The Outside – You Don't Need To Do It Alone

"You can't get to courage without walking through vulnerability."
- Brene Brown

I remember the day like it was yesterday. I had just left my full-time career and was struggling with depression but was starting to pick myself up and require more from myself. Dreading the messages from friends and fellow fitness professionals wondering where I was and if I was ok I decided to go on to Facebook. That was when an advertisement for The Institute For The Psychology of Eating, founded by Marc David showed up on the screen. I researched it and I had a strong pull in my heart. The program was designed to support people who struggle with Chronic Dieting, Binge Eating, Body Image, and so much more. I could tell it was different from anything I had done (or seen) before. I enrolled in the certification and began to dive deep into the psychology behind why people struggle with food the way they do in the world – what thoughts, feelings, and beliefs they are carrying that may no longer be supporting them but in fact harming them. I was able to learn about mind-body nutrition and how essential it is to find pleasure in food and address the beautiful connection between the body and the mind. Receiving the title of a Certified Eating Psychology Coach (which is now referred to as a Mind Body Eating Coach) by the Institute was a very important part of my personal journey and allows me to support my clients with long term support including truly a holistic approach to honoring the mind, body, and spirit.

My Friendships Have Changed. I am blessed to have created a beautiful circle of friends that truly love and support me. It has reminded me to never try and do life alone. It is so important to have friends that you can confide in, laugh with, shed some tears, celebrate each other's successes, and play with. You will be surrounded by energy that will fill your cup up with overflowing love. Take the time to reflect on your relationships and see where you need to make some changes that will move you forward in your life.

I have found that journaling, meditation, and moving my body has been essential in getting me where I am today. Writing down all my fears, joys, misunderstandings, and dreams onto paper has allowed me to honor my emotions, instead of burying my feelings. There are lessons in them if we allow ourselves to listen and honor without judgment. Meditation has helped me create space in my mind for the answers I need in my life to have time to surface and be heard. And being able to CHOOSE how I want to move my body each day has been so incredibly healing. I know firsthand that moving your body helps to shift emotions but sometimes that will mean yoga or a walk in the woods with my Golden Retriever while other times it means strength training or a great sweat in a cardio class. There are no rules on what I must do – I get to choose by asking my body what she needs from me today.

Learning from others whether it is from books, podcasts, or attending self-development retreats has taught me so much about myself. Sharing my story from stages has been incredibly healing as well as it released the shame I have been carrying for so long. This is where I challenged my limiting beliefs, perfectionism and worthiness by going face to face with my ego. I will also add that attending these types of events has brought incredible people into my life that I would never have had the chance to meet. If you want to create a circle of people you connect with – you need to go and find them because they are out there!

My Non-Negotiables Moving Forward

1. Breaking Up with The Scale

This was pivotal in my journey. The day I said that I would no longer stand on a scale again to tell me if I was 'good enough' was the day that I truly started living again. My mental health changed immediately. Instead of stripping down to nothing and allowing a piece of metal to determine my happiness, I choose to count my blessings and focus on gratitude each morning. Now I am truly living and choosing ME every day. I do not need to be fixed – my body was never the problem.

2. No More Diets or Quick Fixes

I made a conscious decision to stop trying to intentionally lose weight. No more tracking, measuring, or rules around when or what foods I can eat. I have learned to tune into my body and get to know what it intuitively needs each day. This allows me to make choices that are best for me and my health and not feel like a failure when I can't follow the rules of a diet. They are not sustainable and set people up for binging and restrictive eating. This ultimately leads to more self-defeating thoughts impacting the body, mind, and spirit. I have found that having more freedom and not labeling foods as good or bad and instead focusing on the nourishment that foods provide has allowed me to not feel out of control. I now get to choose, and I do so consciously every day!

3. Don't Give Up When It Gets Hard

I know that life is not meant to be easy. Just as there were big lessons in my life up until this point, I know that there will be more to come. I know my eating disorder's voice will show up when I least expect her to. She may show up as a perfectionist, or the health-conscious fanatic who tells me I need to be stricter with my food. But I know in my heart that I get to be in charge of what my life looks like and feels like, no one gets to tell me otherwise. So, I will be ready to use my voice. It took me a long time to find it, but I now know that I have a lot of wisdom to share with myself and words to inspire and impact others.

How I Use My Life Lessons To Help Others

As a Food Freedom & Mindset Coach, I am passionate about helping women heal their relationships with food and body image as well as help them create a mindset that supports them so that they can truly step into their lives and live their deeper purpose but most importantly find JOY in every day. Comparison and Perfectionism and the belief "I am good enough" are real challenges that are affecting women's quality of life and mental health. Throughout life, women are being influenced in different ways through their family upbringing, media, and diet culture that their bodies need to be different in order to be accepted and loved. This leaves women grasping for hope by jumping into every new diet fad, pill, or potion which ultimately leaves them feeling that they will never measure up. As an online coach for groups, one to one coaching and as a Certified Elite Speaker, I am using eating psychology and mind-body nutrition strategies to help women improve their mindset so that they can move forward in their lives. What I have learned and continue to implement in my life is not meant for me to keep to myself but, to share & teach. Not only the pretty stuff but also the messy stuff that shows up along the way. Life is not about getting to the destination but learning how to surf the waves that show up along the way. When we realize that life is happening for us not to us it's a game-changer!

You get one chance at life and I wish you nothing but love and grace as you learn to navigate it. And remember you don't need to do life alone. In fact, you will go farther when you link arms with others who want the best for you.

About the Author

Kim shares the lessons she learned in her 30 year-long fight with disordered eating, eating disorders, and her struggles with self-acceptance, all occurring simultaneously with her 25+ years in the fitness industry.

Her training at the Institute for the Psychology of Eating enables her to use a mind-body centered approach to nutrition as well as cutting edge eating psychology strategies. Through her programs, coaching, and speaking events for women, Kim teaches the necessary steps to finding food freedom and guides you towards your path to healing and self-acceptance. She empowers women to step fully into their lives and release their inner critic, freeing up mental space to go after all of their dreams, free from comparison and perfectionism.

Food Freedom & Mindset Coach

Website:
www.kimbasler.com

Email:
kim@kimbasler.com

Facebook:
Kim Basler Food Freedom & Mindset Coach

Instagram:
KimBasler_FoodFreedom

LinkedIn:
https://www.linkedin.com/in/kim-basler-22a14827/

Tragedy, Truth and Triumph

By Lynn Tanguay

C reating my lifestyle business was not my original goal but the vision and reality from the needs I see day in and day out with my personal training clients. The original plan was to build a successful fitness studio with personal training clients and small group classes. I'm passionate about fitness and nutrition because that was the driving force I used to change my life and situation. It's fulfilling and empowering to help others create a healthier lifestyle through fitness and nutrition.

After having my son, I didn't want to go back into the grind of the corporate world; I wanted to have a more flexible schedule. While on maternity leave, my fitness studio was built and opened for business. I have had great success with this portion of my business. After three years I really saw the need for more than workout routines and nutritional plans. My clients would have great success until life's unexpected hiccups happened; be it a shift in their jobs, a change in their relationships, a change in their health. The old habits and self-sabotage would start creeping back in. I decided to hire a professional mindset coach and embark on a year of learning and educating myself on how to bring this into my programs. Having the ability to help my clients shift their mindsets opened up a new world for them. Working with women who are exhausted, overwhelmed, unappreciated, and who have just decided "this is how life is going to be" is not okay with me. We work closely together to create a healthier, happier lifestyle, and the best version of ourselves through self-love, empowerment, letting shit go, and finding fulfilment.

Who I am today is far different than who I used to be. I have spent the last fifteen years creating the life I want, knowing I deserved it, and now paying it forward by helping others do the same.

I was a party girl from college days right up until I was thirty. Always ready for a fun time with friends and always ready for the next adventure. I was also a man saver. The kind who picks a man who has a ton of baggage and then decides on being the one to save them. I had no idea what direction I was going in and I was always too busy saving "the man" to focus on my future and my goals. I didn't give much thought or focus on what I wanted to create in my life because I honestly didn't know.

When I was 24 years old my world came crashing down around me when my dad committed suicide. My dad had been diagnosed with Bipolar for ten years prior to this, with things going downhill quickly after. Things were done and said that tore our family apart and in the end, I feel that the guilt and shame became unbearable for him. Losing the one man in my life that genuinely loved me for me, who always had a hug, wink, or smile for me, who always made me feel special was gone forever...Even now, twenty years later, my heart still aches, and tears flow when I think of the incredible pain he must have been in to take his own life.

My life virtually spiraled out of control after losing my dad. I was preoccupied with taking care of my mom who was the one who discovered him, helping her try and cope with the harsh reality that she was now dealing with after losing the love of her life. I was busy making sure my siblings were okay. I was busy making sure I wasn't heard or seen crying because I had to be the strong one. I was never angry, just incredibly sad, hurt, confused, and filled with regret for all the words that were never said and all the words that I did say and would never be able to take back.

Years of avoiding the "issues" were chased with lots of drinking to numb the pain and blur my reality. Years of abusing my body with unhealthy foods, unhealthy habits; overeating, starving myself, diet pills, excessive exercise, trying to find some control over the uncontrollable circumstances around me. Years of being in a relationship with someone who was emotionally unavailable, someone who used my weaknesses against me to do as he pleased and bring me down even further down the dark hole. This vicious cycle continued for five years. The patterns were always the same and literally stuck on repeat. The guys were different, the alcohol of choice was different, my physical health was different, the locations were different BUT the end result was always the same.

I found myself curled up in a ball on the floor of my closet one morning crying hysterically, thinking, How the hell did I end up here? I was so lonely, so sad, so hurt, so embarrassed by the mess my life was in, emotionally and physically. This was not the life I wanted to live.

In that instant I knew I couldn't keep doing this, I was so unhappy with my life and my circumstances. I will never forget the feeling that came over me in that closet. I had ENOUGH, I was no longer willing to live this way. I have to credit my dad for giving me the strength to wipe my tears, get off that floor, and start creating the life I knew he would have wanted for me.

I have not stopped moving forward since that day. Once I decided I deserved more, my journey of self-discovery started; learning to love myself, taking responsibility for my actions and my choices, understanding I was worthy, and deserving of living a happy and healthy life on my terms was the driving force for all the amazing things to come. I left North Carolina and moved back to Vermont to be close to my family and friends who were my amazing support team, I ended a very toxic relationship, I stopped drinking to numb the pain, I started working out and running, I started eating nutritional foods, I started laughing again, and I started taking care of myself. I started feeling hope and light on my face and heart.

Believing in myself and knowing I am capable of anything was the flood gate that opened all possibilities. I want people to know and understand there is a different path, a different outcome than the one they feel stuck in. We all have choices and we all have opportunities. What we do about our circumstances is a difference in staying stuck or creating the life we want and truly deserve.

I believe it was my dad's work that I met my husband and I know he was guiding me to the next chapter of my life. Once

I was able to put into words what I wanted in a man and be open with my heart, I met my husband. He has been the biggest influencer and supporter in helping me create the success I have had in my business and personal life. Having someone by your side each and every day encouraging you, acknowledging all your hard work, praising you with kind words, and showing you with his actions how special you are has been what fuels me to keep improving myself and having the best life possible.

Putting all the darkness behind me has been a fifteen-year journey. I no longer look at the past as something I want to forget but I embrace the lessons I have learned and the hurt I went through to become the person I am today. With determination, strength, and love I found myself, my purpose, and my mission. My life is not full of rainbows and sunshine and I still have times that I struggle. What is different now is that I am able to acknowledge, recognize, and evaluate the issues and spend my energy finding solutions instead of drama and excuses.

Creating daily tools that I am able to practice keeps me front and center with my emotional well-being, my physical well-being, and my spiritual well-being. Having a daily self-care routine through fueling my body with amazing nutrition, moving my body with weights and cardio helps me to stay energized, focused, and strong. Practicing gratitude every day keeps me grounded in the now and appreciate all that I have. Letting others know how thankful I am for them makes my heart happy. Lifting others up instead of knocking them down feeds my soul. Spending time with my loved ones making memories laughing and enjoying each other's company completes me.

The biggest life changer has been the shift in my mindset. When you learn to shift your mindset from fixed to growth, your perspective on your choices, situations, opportunities, and relationships will change.

My five tips on choosing success over darkness are:

1) Take control of your choices and actions.

2) Understand your value, your worth, and always work on changing your limiting beliefs.

3) Raise your standards for what you deserve in your life.

4) Embrace "Fear" and step outside your comfort zone.

5) Lift others up with your words and actions.

Taking control of my shit, stopping the blaming of others, and no longer playing the victim made me realize how strong I was and that I was capable of anything. I was the one in the driver's seat and how I showed up every day was how the world was going to treat me. I was not going to allow others to treat me poorly... I was worth the effort to eat healthily and be physically fit. I was beautiful inside and out. I had amazing qualities as a person. I was learning to love who I was and made sure my limiting beliefs were met with positive affirmations that help shift my way of thinking about myself.

My standards were raised meaning others would treat me the way I allowed them to treat me. Others would also respect me the way I respect myself, and others would love me the way I loved myself. People will treat you the way you allow them to treat you. It all starts from within.

Waking up every morning and allowing myself the time and opportunity to lift weights and get a sweaty cardio session done makes me feel amazing and sets the pace for my entire day. Allowing myself time and space to sit quietly each night and write in my gratitude journal keeps me in check with what I have and how grateful I am for all of it.

Understanding I can say no to obligations or new projects if I feel that I am too busy, or it does not speak to me, without feeling any guilt. These are just some of the things for myself I do, to keep me in that positive mindset, where I function the best.

I no longer hear the nasty little voice in my head telling me "I'm not worth it", "you can't do that", or "what makes you special?" Instead, I have an arsenal of positive affirmations that I use daily to keep my head in the right place and to keep my self-assurance and confidence at a high level. There are times that I can hear that nasty little voice creeping in but instead of wallowing in it and allowing it to suck me under, I use the tools I have learned to flick that switch and change the conversation in my head from negative to positive.

I show up in the world as someone who radiates a positivity for life, love, and laughter. I leave people in a better place emotionally and physically after spending time with me. That is my greatest gift, having someone walk away from me feeling happier and having a spring in their step because they understand that there are choices and opportunities to create the life they want and deserve.

Fear holds people in situations, circumstances, or ruts ... call it what you will, but being fearful and staying in your comfort zone will keep you stuck. Being able to harness that fear and learning it's okay to jump in with both feet and it's accepting that it is okay to fail. Not trying or not doing anything feels like a bigger risk of failure. Growth happens when you push yourself outside your comfort zone and you never know where that is going to take you.

Making a difference in someone's life, I believe is the greatest honor and gift. It's not just about you, it's about lifting others up instead of knocking them down, reaching a handout, and helping others up. We all have that opportunity with our daily actions and conversations. Be the one to inspire, support, and help someone that needs a boost, a hug, or simply just a smile.

One of the most important lessons I learned from losing my dad is that life continues no matter what. Show up each and every day, take action, create an impact, and inspire others. When going through a challenging time be honest with yourself. What are you going to do to change your situation? What type of solution are you wanting? Ask for help and start taking little steps to create action.

When circumstances are ongoing and life continues to pull backward, remind yourself that this too shall pass, this will not be forever. Find a solution to the problem and have an action plan. Remind yourself what you are thankful and grateful for and do something that makes you feel amazing; getting outside and enjoying nature, calling a friend, or getting a massage.

I intend to help others create the lifestyle they want and deserve. When you feel hopeless, alone, and have no idea how to create change, I want you to understand, you always have a choice to change. You are worth it, you are strong, you are special, and you are not alone, I am right here cheering you on and waiting for you to succeed.

My purpose and mission are to educate, support, and inspire women to live their best life possible being the best version of themselves. I was so lost when I started my journey, but the right people came into my life to help me when I needed help. I sought out people who inspired me and I chose to learn from them. I surrounded myself with a tribe of amazing incredible people who paid it forward and gave me back more than they will ever realize.

I am building a community where you will experience love, support, and accountability from like-minded women who have broken the chains that held them in place, the Freedom Fighters.

We are creating a ripple effect and paying it forward.

Are ready to break the cycle, climb out of that rut, and stop the vicious cycle? You can break the cycle.

My lessons have been difficult and painful. I wouldn't change the path I had to take. My lessons have allowed me to become confident, strong, and compassionate and in turn, I am paying it forward to help others do the same in their lives.

The life I have created since taking on the mindset piece and all of the mindset work is what has truly allowed me to create a completely different life not just professionally but personally, as a mom, and a wife.

About the Author

Lynn Tanguay is a Self-Coach, Mindset Motivator and personal trainer. She coaches and mentors people to make physical and emotional transformations in their lives through fitness, nutrition and mindset.

Having overcame life-altering losses of her own with the sudden death of her father from suicide; she has spent the last 15 years Creating the life she wanted and deserved. Lynn learned first hand how important and powerful the following key components are in life: Self love, empowerment, letting go of your story and finding fulfillment. Lynn is now on a mission to educate, support and inspire others to live their best life possible from the inside out.

To contact me please email lynntanguaylifestyle@gmail.com

Check out my website at:

www.LynnTanguaylifestyle.com

Breaking the Silence

By Thembeka Ntuli

It took me so long to be able to say out loud "I WAS ABUSED" because every time I tried to face it, I just wanted to run and hide.

I held onto the shame and fear. I had that childish feeling with me that somehow, I did something bad. That I was bad. That I was shameful. How crazy is it that even as adults that feeling keeps us silent?

As adults we know we didn't do anything wrong. We know that if we ever came across a child being abused we would never shame or blame them. We would help them, no questions asked. We would hold the abuser accountable. It's hard for me to understand why this feeling didn't change for me sooner.

Why did it take me so long to look at all the haters and judgmental people and say I do not own this shame? I was abused and it was wrong. It was even more wrong that all the signs were ignored.

It was wrong that no one stepped in to help me recover. All those adults in my life: teachers, parents, friends' parents... all sat and did nothing. Maybe they didn't know what to do.

The sexual abuse I endured led to human trafficking. I have relived it mentally over and over and truthfully I still do to this day. Counseling as a child or in my earlier years could have done me wonders and possibly saved me from so many feelings of shame and failure in my life.

It is hard for me to understand how past generations chose to ignore everything that was happening. I can't explain or understand how they believed that sexual assault, rape, and abuse of a child wasn't a huge deal or epidemic.

Even now, it seems, we are still in a battle to put a stop to all the ignorance. I am so thankful I have learned to say,

I was abused.

I was ignored.

I suffered tremendously.

I can say this all now with no more fear or shame.

My story is not an easy story to read or understand, yet it is so important for me to share it with the world. I know my story can help someone else with their story. The abuse began when I met my mother for the first time after fourteen years. I was raised by my grandparents. Growing up, I knew my mother rejected me and tried to harm me when I was three months old and that's why I lived with my grandparents. When I finally met her, I was at my grandparent's funeral which happened to be on the same day, as they passed away in the same week but different days. The first person to pass away was my grandmother and she died as a result of diabetes. It was on a Wednesday. My grandfather passed away two days later from a heart attack.

After I lost my grandparents, my mother appeared. She was like a stranger to me. I had no idea how to behave or what I was supposed to say because the people who were dear to me were gone. After the funeral, I was told I had to move and stay with her. They said, "she is your mother." There was no negotiation or no explanation. It was a very confusing and painful time at my young age.

With no real warning or time to adjust, I had to move to the big city with my mom. I had so many questions that I needed answers for and the only person who could give me those answers was this stranger.

Deep down I was excited about living with my mother. At least now when it was Mother's Day, I would be able to get her a card. I would be able to tell her how much her absence in my life affected me and ask her about my father too. All I wished was to have a relationship with her. Unfortunately, it was not the fairy tale I had dreamt of.

My first experience with my mom involved a lie. The excitement I felt died quickly. She made it clear that she would be telling everyone that she was my big sister and she had to care for me because our parents passed away.

She was married and had been trying to have kids for ten years. Her husband welcomed me to be a part of their family as his sister-in-law. It was all lies. My mother had a lot of anger towards me and continuously called me stupid. She would say horrible things to me on a daily basis and blame me for everything that had gone wrong in her life. At least her husband was giving me attention and would see the good in me, or so I thought. I started trusting him because he was kind and would give me money to buy toiletries and lunch for school. It was our little secret that eventually led to sexual abuse that lasted for several years. When it first happened, I told my mother and she chose not to believe me. Instead, she believed that I was trying to destroy her marriage. All I wanted was to be loved and protected.

The abuse kept happening and I didn't know how to stop it. When I was 16 years old, I got pregnant with his child and was taken by my mother to terminate the pregnancy. Things blew up between my mother and her husband. My mother decided to pack her bags and left me with him. The church women were sent to come and pray for me because she thought her daughter was demon-possessed and sleeping around with men. No one knew that I was abused and I believed that no one cared. I had no one to trust. If I reported it I wondered, who was going to protect me?

I could never understand why I was never wanted by my mother. Eventually, I found out the truth about my roots. My mother never knew who my father was. I was the product of a gang-rape when she was in university. Maybe there was too much pain in my conception? She used to tell me "I hated being pregnant with you." "It was such an embarrassment for me and my family." It was obvious she never wanted me.

Eventually, my mom came back, and on the 15th of September of 2013, she sent me to the shop to get bread. I knew something was off because she never sent me so late and I knew we already had some. I had been planning to leave them, and move out on my own. Their biggest threat was that I was going to expose them. I had already started to fight back.

That day outside of our flats, I was kidnapped. They drove around with me until we got to a place in another province. The main purpose of my kidnapping was to be trafficked to

Thailand. I had been bought already to be delivered to the buyer but there were some delays. I was held captive, drugged, prostituted, beaten, chained, and starved. Two other girls were there, one older than me and one younger. I don't know what happened to the older girl but the younger girl and I were rescued. I, unfortunately, learned after that she had ended her own life.

I hoped once I was rescued that my mother was going to see me at the hospital but she never came. The police asked about my mother and her husband and I gave them their address and phone numbers. The statement they gave the police was shocking. They told lies that I was with my boyfriend and didn't tell them. I decided I had to tell the police the truth about my mother and her husband and the abuse.

I learned that the kidnapping had all been a setup. It was all planned. They were arrested but I was made to drop the charges and re-write that my statement was a lie. When I was discharged from the hospital, I had no home and no place to go.

I moved to a recovering center for a few months. Then I was on my own. I moved from place to place, working as a helper just to have a place I could call home.

To survive these ordeals, I developed two strategies. One was to become as invisible as possible so as not to attract any attention and two was to excel at everything I did to prove my worth. I was determined to search for my purpose on earth and start building my dreams. I looked around for resources. I started sharing my story with strangers with the belief that someone would listen to me and the plans I had for the future and offer some help. I allowed myself to be vulnerable and someone listened. It worked. I was given an opportunity to live in a safe place and go back to college and further my studies. Things continued to get better. I learned to be hopeful in everything that I did.

I started to see opportunities because I changed my mindset. I became a top learner at school. I applied for bursaries and leadership grants and I received one to study business administration, and I jumped at it. I applied within the last two days for a three-year bursary that was being advertised on Facebook. I was rewarded with it. I saw opportunities and I went after them. Excitement is what you feel when you work hard and prove to yourself that you do deserve better and you are a survivor! I went through hell and eventually came out on fire with a burning passion to create change.

In my time at the safe house, I have been surrounded by women and their children who have escaped abusive situations. As a victim of child abuse and human trafficking, I understand fully the emotions and feelings that fear, anxiety, and repulsion cause.

During those years of silence, I felt ashamed of myself. I believed it was my fault. That I would be ridiculed and repulsed if I reported it. The driving force behind my silence was fear...fear that he would show up and threaten me...fear that nobody would believe me, fear I would be pitied instead of supported. The trauma and shame of these experiences can run so deep. Sometimes we just want it all to end. I struggled to love myself.

What I have learned and realized is that being silent about your experiences doesn't help your healing and it doesn't empower other survivors to tell their stories. We can all learn to break the silence and regain our personal power.

When one of us somehow finds the courage to speak up, people will begin to listen and they too will stand up for their rights.

Sharing what had happened to me became incredibly liberating. I regained my power and sense of self-worth. I felt a pure sense of freedom and something that felt close to healing and lasting peace. Everyone deserves healing, freedom, and peace.

I am very grateful to all the women who have come to my rescue and mothered me to be this young powerful and inspiring woman.

So, here's some good news...

You Can Change Your Life and Create Your Own Destiny.

Change is possible! We can all transform and change our lives for the better by tapping into potential locked away within each and every one of us. The key is to have greater self- awareness, and understanding who we really are. I always saw myself as an inspiration to others and as a successful person. When I was a child I had goals and dreams. As a result of my experiences, abuse, being trafficked, abandonment, homelessness, and rejection, nothing seemed possible. It is not easy to start all over after you have lost everything, yet it is possible if deep inside you believe you have what it takes. I had to be strong and pull myself together, to stay focused. I kept telling myself "One day you will get out of this situation." And that's exactly what happened eventually.

Be hopeful in everything that you do and have hope when you make decisions! That's what I did; I already saw the future before it began because I was tired of being stuck in my past. I demanded that my present be the future I always dreamed about.

So what now?

This is the question I ask myself.

I have a place to live, I am safe, and I'm studying. What now?

People are searching and looking for answers and maybe I could be a help to them, I thought...

So what can you do? Where can you begin?

Forgiving yourself.

Before you can help others you must help yourself first. I had to learn how to forgive not only the people who have hurt me but to forgive myself. In order to set myself free. What the abuser did to me was wrong. None of us ever deserve it. The guilt, shame, and fear are not where your energy belongs right now, or ever again. Out of all the things that you deserve, self-forgiveness is towards the top of the list. Abuse in any form is never your fault. It doesn't matter who the person was. It doesn't matter how they got into your life. It doesn't matter how long the relationship was. It doesn't matter why you stayed. None of that matters, but here's what does:

You made it through. You survived. You're free. You did it.

Take your time.

Maybe you've been told you were not 'allowed' to hang out with a certain friend, told that your long-term dream was a waste of time, or otherwise constantly questioned and controlled on the who, what, when, where, or why of how you spent your time. Being out of that relationship or situation can often feel more frightening than freeing and that is completely normal.

There is no time limit on healing. Yet, you decide that.

Your life is your own to live, and you can take as much time as you want, or move as quickly as you want. You can focus on what you want, who you want to surround yourself with, and where, when, and how you want to do it.

Self-care on your own terms.

What do you love to do? Do you know? Start to write those things down. What about that slam book club you've always wanted to join? Or maybe getting the pet you've wanted for years. Maybe chasing that dream job across the country. It can be a small desire or a big one.

Do one small thing every day that brings you joy.

Don't let anything hold you back.

Re-draw your boundaries.

Setting healthy boundaries allows you to feel more empowered and less stressed. It allows for fresh mental space and time to surround ourselves with people who support us. For me, part of healing means recognizing that my needs matter and that they are my responsibility. I can choose who and what I surround myself with. So can you.

The power is in your hands.

Take back your story.

Rebuilding your story is a highly personal step. It can feel like an awakening, and can also be very emotionally difficult to process as you peel back the layers of your story. That is a very important process though to be able to move through it, into a new story.

Regardless of where you take your story from here, all the choices are yours now. Everyone heals at their own time. Your journey can take on many different directions as you address each part of your situation, and there are resources available at each and every step of the way.

Above all, know that you are loved and that you are not alone.

Enuf with Woman and Child abuse Movement.

#SurvivorsVoice.

In 2017 I took a powerful first step and created a survivor's voice movement. I was finding the courage to share my story. Enuf was born as a result of my journey from victim to victor.

The movement aims to help other survivors of Gender-based violence and human trafficking, encouraging them not to give up on their dreams and instead to have HOPE.

Secondly, I wanted to create a platform for women around the world who would resonate with that purpose. I am filled with passion and excitement for the journey that is unfolding.

Because of the years of therapy, loving support from the home and friends, and Enuf, I have finally arrived at a place where I no longer need substances, food, or other "highs" to mask the pain resulting from the abuse. I have learned many,

many things from my experiences, and as a survivor of human trafficking.

Regardless of what you've experienced in your life, or what others think, or say or ignore about it, you can and deserve to be heard and to heal.

I imagine that in the years ahead I will even learn even more from other people, by speaking up, sharing our stories, and being the voices that cannot speak for themselves.

About the Author

Thembeka Ntuli is an activist against human trafficking and gender-based violence. She is a final year student studying a diploma in Marketing Management. She also a founder of Enuf against Women and Child abuse movement which supports fellow survivors and victims to find HOPE.

Radical Responsibility Became the Light in my Dark Life

By Marsha Vanwynsberghe

Years ago, my life looked vastly different from the life I live today. At that time, it was dark, filled with sadness, loneliness, and a mixture of comparison, jealousy, anger and resentment. There was little joy, happiness, or spark. None of this was a recipe to create change, and sadly I was the one making the recipe. I was waiting for someone else to come and fix my life. Someone else had to have the answer because I didn't.

I blamed everyone, including myself for where my life was at. Ownership didn't exist yet. I didn't even know of the word. It wasn't until years later that I realized that ownership and blame couldn't live in the same place.

I was alone, isolated, and praying for someone would bring me a solution. I thought if I could just get stronger or be stronger or pray harder or be nicer, then I could fix our mess.

Being stronger didn't matter. It had nothing to do with strength.

Years of dealing with teen substance abuse with our boys left me feeling hopeless, stuck, and destined for a life of walking on eggshells wondering if or when the next bomb would drop, because we all knew it would drop. Our life had reached the point that school, sports, family, mental well-being and living arrangements had all been impacted and affected. I didn't know what to do next or where to go. I was at an all-time low in my life. I hated where my life was at and I hated myself for letting it get to this point. I took full responsibility for everything and everyone's behavior and choices. I spent all my energy trying to "fix" everyone around me.

I vividly remember sitting on the floor after almost losing both boys only days apart (one to an attempted suicide and one to an overdose), screaming and sobbing, "Why is this my life? Why am I being punished? What did I do that was so wrong?"

I made it all about me and I just couldn't seem to see anything outside of myself. That's what pain can do sometimes; it leaves you feeling very self-centered as a victim, and honestly, life as a victim is one fast way for nothing to change.

Then as I sat there on the floor, I heard a voice saying, STOP. Over and over again, I heard it loud and clear, saying STOP. Stop what? How could I stop something that I wasn't doing? We were here because of the choices our kids were making. That's the story I kept telling myself.

Deep down I knew what STOP meant. I knew the answer. I had to stop trying to fix, manage, and control everything around me. I had to take ownership of myself. At this point, I didn't even understand the word ownership.

Years ago, a counselor had said that if the boys decided to come back to us, that I had to be a springboard for them. At that point, I was a messy pile of quicksand. I couldn't be a springboard for myself let alone anyone else. I had to learn to be the springboard in my own life.

It didn't happen overnight. It felt like it took months to make this adjustment, yet it was also a change that happened in an instant. As soon as I understood the word 'choice', I realized that I had a choice, and I somehow had forgotten along the way.

I had a choice in how I responded to what was happening in my life. In fact, we all did.

This was the start of learning about radical responsibility, and the start of me taking radical responsibility for myself. I couldn't OWN my story if I didn't OWN my choices or if I didn't take radical responsibility for myself.

I learned to keep life simple, by only taking ownership for my choices. I was done taking responsibility for what my kids were or were not doing. Every time I owned their choices it meant that they didn't have to, and I came to the realization very quickly that two people couldn't own a decision at the same time. When I owned their choices, I also owned their consequences, and no one will change their behaviour or actions when there isn't a consequence. It was so humbling to realize that I actually was contributing to the problems. I was adding fuel to our situation. I owned the fact that my choices were making our lives worse. As soon as I saw that, I stopped blaming them for their decisions. Here's the kicker...I was blaming them for everything that was or wasn't happening in my own life because I wasn't taking any ownership of my life. Yikes! I had to stop blaming them for the stress in my life, the stress in my business, my marriage, my workplace, my health, my weight gain, my lack of fitness and health, my inability to eat well, my lack of sleep, I could go on and on. It was time for me to own my choices, literally, own all my choices, and that is the exact opposite of blame. Once I let go of blame, I felt a massive weight lift off my shoulders and the fog lifted. Life became so much clearer and simpler.

- I was responsible for myself.

- I could own my own choices.

- I was on a path that was leading me back to myself.

- I actually had the answers all along, I simply didn't see it before.

At the end of the day, my life was up to me, and it was so freeing to recognize that it was exactly the same thing that my boys would have to do on their journey. They were responsible for their choices and what they chose to create for their life. It was their life after all. It was so ironic because even before I had kids, I would always say, "I am not raising my kids to keep them, they're not mine to keep. They are mine to raise to send out into the world. What they create is up to them." Now it was time to actually live by my own words and let them live their own journey. .

So how did I get from the space of being on the floor to having a few realizations about ownership, to actually creating a business from sharing my story to helping other women do the same? It definitely wasn't a straight line. I didn't know what I was creating at the time, I simply knew I wanted to create something different from what I was living. That way of living had to stop because I wasn't living at all and everyone was suffering from my choices, especially myself.

First, I had to learn what vulnerability meant and how to practice it. It was scary as hell to share my fears and insides with everyone. I was scared, beyond scared, yet I knew I had to share. I felt like my story was eating me alive and by sharing it, I could start the healing process. Around this time, I read the book, "Love Warrior" by Glennon Doyle, and "Daring Greatly" by Brene Brown and I could see the power of sharing my story and how it could help others. I started with a couple of Facebook posts in a closed group and gradually moved it to my own social media. Then, I started sharing my message from the stage through speaking engagements, on CBC radio, and in parent support groups. I never set out to start a business. I set out to help someone else who felt alone on their journey.

I felt pulled to write a book. This is where it all started for me. 12 months of writing, editing, planning, and my book "When She Stopped Asking Why" was born. The reason for the title was simple and it came to me suddenly one day. The turning point came when I decided to stop asking the word "why". For years, I repeatedly asked myself, "Why me? Why us? and why them?" As if I was expecting an answer that would make sense and justify our chaos. Did it actually matter? Was there any possible answer that would make all this suffering worth it? The word 'why' was a victim question and I decided to completely strike it from my vocabulary. Victim questions keep us stuck looking and waiting for someone else to fix it or give us the solutions. While I sat waiting for an answer, I completely took my own power away from myself because I wasn't moving or getting into action. We can find the answers when we get into action and start moving. We will never find them standing still. The word why had to go.

My intention for the book was simple. I wanted it to be a source of support and provide answers for others who had never walked a day in my shoes. I shared my story of how I went from point A to B, from pain to purpose and as a result, it ended up being a source of support and principles for others who were struggling in their own stories. We are all more alike than different. We are connected by pain, emotions, and most importantly, our stories.

Stories became the word that connected the dots in the business that was forming.

Women were stuck in their stories. Stories that no longer served them, that kept them stuck and small in their lives and ultimately stories that they had outgrown. These stories served a purpose and the women that were reaching out to me kept asking me questions such as:

- How do I learn to share a story?

- How do I move forward, let go of what it was supposed to be like, and create a new ending?

- How do I learn to stand ON my story instead of staying stuck IN it replaying it over and over?

- How do I find the gifts in my story, the lessons I am meant to share with others?

- How do I learn to embrace vulnerability, share my story, and use it to help others, like I was doing?

- How do I find the courage to share my story and be that voice or light to support others?

This was the ripple effect that I had always dreamed of being a part of!

The opportunity to share my story to help others create change in their life actually became the fuel to keep going. Creating purpose from our chaos made it all make sense.

Over time the Radical Responsibility Mastermind was born, and this created the space to allow women to work together, collaborate and connect, to support each other and a chance to help even more women with their stories. Teaching women to call out their stories, take full ownership for their stories and learning how to stand on their stories became my fuel and purpose. I never set out for this to be a business at all. I simply gave it space to grow, room to breathe and the opportunities presented themselves to me.

Do I wish that I could have learned the lessons in a simpler, and less painful manner? Absolutely! That is not how this story unfolds. It has happened exactly how it was supposed to, and I learned first-hand that the road of struggle can eventually become the road of growth. I am grateful for the lessons as I wouldn't have learned them without living them. This journey has allowed me to be in the space of creating this collaborative book, "Owning Your Choices", featuring 8 women from across the world who are sharing their stories of courage as they found their way back to themselves by simply owning their choices. Our message can reach places we never imagined. To this day I still receive monthly royalty payments for my book in Japan. That is every single month for almost 3 years. My story also led to me starting a podcast called, "Own Your Choices, Own Your Life", and that podcast was heard by a girl in South Africa, Thembeka, who is currently a part of this collaborative book.

We never know where our story will land and who is literally praying for the solutions that we are holding onto. If my story helps someone else find the courage to share their story, then I will continue to share it and impact other women. Learning to call OUT our stories, learning to OWN our stories, and learning how to stand ON our stories instead of IN them, gives us back our personal power. We can make the greatest impact when we start in our own lives first. I am driven to helping women take Radical Responsibility for their stories to create a massive impact on the world. This journey has brought the most incredible women into my life, women I would have otherwise never had the privilege of meeting. For that, I am eternally grateful.

Are you ready to learn how to stand on your story and be the change you wish to see in the world? The world is waiting for you.

About the Author

Marsha is the 6-time Bestselling Author of "When She Stopped Asking Why". She shares her lessons as a parent who dealt with teen substance abuse far past the level of normal experimentation.

Through her programs, coaching, podcast, and live events for women, Marsha teaches the power of Radical Responsibility and Owning Your Choices in your own life. She empowers women how to own their stories and use the lessons to build platform businesses that impact, serve and support others.

https://www.marshavanw.com
https://www.facebook.com/marshavanwynsberghe
https://www.instagram.com/marshavanw

Own Your Choices Own Your Life Podcast:
https://ownyourchoicesownyourlife.libsyn.com/rss

Stay Connected

1. **Marsha Vanwynsberghe**

https://marshavanw.com
https://www.facebook.com/marshavanwynsberghe
https://www.instagram.com/marshavanw
https://www.linkedin.com/in/marshavanwynsberghe/

2. **Marisa Lupo**

https://marisalupocoaching.com/
https://www.facebook.com/marisalupocoaching/
https://www.instagram.com/marisalupocoaching

3. **Kim Basler**

https://www.kimbasler.com
https://www.facebook.com/kim.basler
https://www.instagram.com/kimbasler_foodfreedom/

4. **Lynn Tanguay**

https://www.lynntanguaylifestyle.com
https://www.facebook.com/lynn.tanguay.3

5. **Kelly Thorne**

https://www.kellyjanecoaching.com

https://www.facebook.com/kellyjanethorne
https://www.instagram.com/kellyjanecoaching
https://www.facebook.com/groups/findingfreedomfromwithin

6. Tinya Gray

www.tinya.love
https://www.facebook.com/twtinya
https://www.linkedin.com/in/tinya/

7. Thembeka Ntuli

https://www.facebook.com/profile.php?id=100007265087274
https://www.instagram.com/?hl=en
https://m.facebook.com/ThandekaEnuf/?_rdr

8. Shannon Matthews

https://www.instagram.com/_shannonismakingthingshappen_/

www.ingramcontent.com/pod-product-compliance
Lightning Source LLC
LaVergne TN
LVHW020936090426
835512LV00020B/3377